W9-AUK-758

This book makes me want to get up and do something. Now. Today.

—**Dr. Kevin Leman,** author of *Have a New Kid by Friday* and *Have a New Husband by Friday*

This book is not only inspiring and thoughtful, but it's a profound challenge to each of us to stop focusing on what we can't do and invest our lives and energies in what we can. *She Did What She Could* is empowering to anyone who has ever asked, "What difference could I possibly make?"

—**Margaret Feinberg,** national speaker and author of *The Sacred Echo* and *Scouting the Divine*

Elisa Morgan has been unleashing power in people for a long time. This book is a little time bomb that will go off when you know your gifts and your limits and say yes to God in the midst of them.

—**John Ortberg,** pastor of Menlo Church and author of *Faith and Doubt*

I loved *She Did What She Could*! What is amazing to me is that one little phrase issues such a profound challenge for the heart and at the same time gives a deep and abiding peace. Thank you, Elisa, for this beautiful Bible teaching and the tender stories that call me to live a great big life, doing what I can today and believing God for what I can do tomorrow.

—**Angela Thomas,** speaker and best-selling author of *Do You Think I'm Beautiful?*

What an empowering book! *She Did What She Could* made me yearn for a deeper, more loving relationship with Jesus. It caused me to take a hard look at what I can do—me, an ordinary woman, profoundly and passionately loved, and to act out of that love. Simply, with a sincere heart. Not to be seen, not out of duty, obligation, or guilt, but to please and serve the One who loved me first. I want to "live loved."

—**Fern Nichols,** founder and president of Moms In Touch International

Elisa Morgan paints a vigorous picture of life on the front lines. This book is a convincing reminder that we all have Kingdom work to do, that the opportunities are all around us, that God is powerfully accomplishing his purposes for the world through us, and that more—much more!—will be accomplished when his sons and daughters serve him together.

—**Carolyn Custis James,** president of Synergy Women's Network, Inc., and author of *The Gospel of Ruth*

I love this book because it challenged me in such a way that I am now compelled to respond. And really, isn't that what we all want in a book? Elisa brilliantly weaves truths from biblical examples into our modern-day opportunities and spurs us on to action. It brings me great joy to recommend this amazing book.

—**Lysa TerKeurst,** speaker, president of Proverbs 31 Ministries and author of *Becoming More Than a Good Bible Study Girl*

She Did What She Could

she did what she could

five words of Jesus that will change your life

Elisa Morgan

TYNDALE
MOMENTUM™

The nonfiction imprint of Tyndale House Publishers, Inc.

Visit Tyndale online at www.tyndale.com.

Visit Tyndale Momentum online at www.tyndalemomentum.com.

TYNDALE, *Tyndale Momentum*, and Tyndale's quill logo are registered trademarks of Tyndale House Publishers, Inc. The Tyndale Momentum logo is a trademark of Tyndale House Publishers, Inc. Tyndale Momentum is the nonfiction imprint of Tyndale House Publishers, Inc., Carol Stream, Illinois.

She Did What She Could: Five Words of Jesus That Will Change Your Life

Copyright © 2009 by Elisa Morgan. All rights reserved.

Designed by Dean H. Renninger

Edited by Susan Taylor

Published in association with the literary agency of Alive Communications, Inc., 7680 Goddard Street, Suite 200, Colorado Springs, CO 80920, www.alivecommunications.com.

Unless otherwise indicated, all Scripture quotations are taken from the *Holy Bible*, New Living Translation, copyright © 1996, 2004, 2007 by Tyndale House Foundation. Used by permission of Tyndale House Publishers, Inc., Carol Stream, Illinois 60188. All rights reserved.

Scripture quotations marked NIV are taken from the Holy Bible, *New International Version*,® *NIV*.® Copyright © 1973, 1978, 1984, 2011 by Biblica, Inc.® Used by permission. All rights reserved worldwide.

For information about special discounts for bulk purchases, please contact Tyndale House Publishers at csresponse@tyndale.com, or call 1-800-323-9400.

Library of Congress Cataloging-in-Publication Data

Morgan, Elisa, date.
    She did what she could (SDWSC) : five words of Jesus that will change your life / Elisa Morgan.
        p. cm.
    Includes bibliographical references.
    ISBN 978-1-4143-3378-6 (hc)
1. Christian women—Religious life. 2. Social justice—Religious aspects—Christianity. 3. Mary, of Bethany, Saint. 4. Bible. N.T. Mark XIV, 3-9—Criticism, interpretation, etc. I. Title.
    BV4527.M635 2009
    241'.677—dc22   2009022879

Repackage first published in 2017 under ISBN 978-1-4964-3227-8.

Printed in the United States of America

23 22 21 20 19 18 17
 7   6   5   4   3   2   1

To the Marys.
You have each shaped my "she."

Contents

Acknowledgments   xi

Introduction   xiii

Part 1: She Did What She Could   1

1   **She** Did What She Could   3

2   She **Did** What She Could   11

3   She Did **What** She Could   15

4   She Did What **She** Could   21

5   She Did What She **Could**   29

6   **She Did What She Could**   35

Part 2: What If I Did What I Could?   39

7   What If . . . **I** Did What I Could?   41

8   What If . . . I **Did** What I Could?   47

9   What If . . . I Did **What** I Could?   55

10   What If . . . I Did What **I** Could?   63

11   What If . . . I Did What I **Could**?   73

12   **What If I Did What I Could?**   81

Part 3: What If We Did What We Could?   87

13   What If . . . **We** Did What **We** Could?   89

14   **What If We Did What We Could?**   99

Afterword   111

STUDY GUIDE 115

INTRODUCTION 117

LESSON ONE:
She Did What She Could 119
A relationship with Jesus results in a response.

LESSON TWO:
Who Did What She Could and Why? 133
Live loved.

LESSON THREE:
What If I Did What I Could? 149
How to live loved.

LESSON FOUR:
What If I Didn't Do What I Could? 163
Live with no regrets.

LESSON FIVE:
What If We Did What We Could? 177
You plus me equals we.

LESSON SIX:
What If We All Did What We Could? 191
The power of "we."

Notes 203
About the Author 205

Acknowledgments

She Did What She Could came to me in a gradual, reverberating ripple until its message lodged itself solidly in my heart and now motivates my every day. I didn't expect it. I didn't ask for it. At times, I'm not sure what to do with it. But I do believe *She Did What She Could* is from God, and my commitment is to seek his leading in its expression and investment.

Others have been tenaciously at my side through the development of the concept, the writing, and the final expression of this book. There were many times when I couldn't seem to move ahead or didn't even know if I was supposed to. I am so grateful for their "picking up a corner of my mat" and taking me to Jesus as the paralytic's friends did for him in Mark 2.

To those who read and advised, thank you for your wise input. Kenna Barron, Valerie Bell, Dr. Craig Blomberg, Carla Foote, Carol Kuykendall, Karen Marchant, Evan Morgan, Naomi Cramer Overton, Kendall Parkhurst, Karen Parks, Shelly Radic, Dr. Liz Selzer, Georgia Skiles, Dr. Brian Stafford, and Philip Yancey, your investment made *She Did What She Could* tighter, clearer, more applicable to more people, and better biblically.

To Rick Christian and Lee Hough, thank you for representing *She Did What She Could* with such passion. And Lee, thank you for your valuable writing input in readying the first draft for the eyes of others.

To my friends at Tyndale—Carol Traver, Sue Taylor, Becky Nesbitt, Maria Eriksen, and Ron Beers—thank you for embracing *She Did What She Could* with your whole hearts. Wow!

And to the board, staff, field leaders, and volunteers of MOPS International, thank you for first receiving the message of *She Did What She Could*, then reproducing it in a movement of individuals whose lives were changed, and now wanting to make others different by SDWSC-ing every single day.

Introduction

Most of us care. We really do. We care about our own lives,
for sure, and also about the lives of those around us. We care
about poverty and injustice, about orphans and the sick. We
care about the folks who live and work alongside us and about
what happens in their families, in their hearts, and in their
heads. And yet, weighed down by everyday responsibilities—
bringing home a paycheck, putting food on the table, shuttling
kids around—we question our ability to make a difference.
When we're bombarded by the latest celebrity-help-the-world-
athon, we shrug our shoulders in futility. *Me? How?* Faced with
the seeming insignificance of what we have to offer, we don't
offer anything.

Maybe it's because we think that in order for it to count,
to make a difference that matters, we have to do something
big, or *everything* we could do, or something no one else
has done.

But that's not true.

The Backstory

What can we do?

I came to ask this question one night while watching the
NBC Nightly News anchored by Brian Williams. My kids were

off doing their own things elsewhere. My husband was traveling. I was sitting on my couch with a stack of files from work by my side and my dinner in front of me on the ottoman. It was a normal night of multitasking: eating dinner, working, and watching the news.

I heard Brian say something about a special report from Ann Curry of the *TODAY* show that was important enough to re-air in the evening. I looked up from my reading as Ann apologized for the pictures she was about to show—not exactly appropriate for the dinner hour. Then she launched into a tale of torture, describing the conditions of special needs adults in Serbia, who were kept in cribs their *entire lives*. Across the screen came pictures of grown men in the fetal position, sucking their thumbs and rocking back and forth in frozen contortions.

"Some of these men have never been released from their beds," Ann commented.

How can this be? I found myself standing in the middle of my family room, hands raised in the air, *howling*. Then a sob erupted, and tears started down my face.

Now, I'm not a stranger to tragedy. I've sat at the bedsides of the elderly as they loosened their grip on their dignity—and on life. I've preached in rescue missions and prisons. I've traveled to Central America, South America, and the Caribbean and have witnessed firsthand the poverty and deep needs of the people there. Once I viewed the head of a horse, discarded by a butcher, in a muddy, rutted row of shacks. Another time I trudged through a jungle to visit a family consisting of three children, the oldest of which was seven years old. I gaped at the four-year-old cook stirring their dinner of beans while shooing flies off its surface. I've seen hard stuff before.

But something cracked me open that night, and like a foot jammed in a doorway, it wouldn't let me close back down.

Do something.

A week later I saw another story of human tragedy on CBS's *60 Minutes*: hundreds of thousands of Congolese women who were victims of multiple rapes.

How can this be?

And then I heard the head of the International Justice Mission, speaking about sex trafficking, say that twenty-seven million people have been sold into forced prostitution.

What?

During these unsettling weeks, as I heard of these soul-troubling tragedies, I had been working my way through a book in which one particular story demanded my return day after day. It wasn't a new tale. Actually, it was one I'd read many, many, *many* times. But in this particular season it somehow grabbed on to my soul, squeezing it tight and wringing from it a reaction that required attention.

The Story
She saw him across the room and immediately sensed a familiar awareness in the very core of her being. It wasn't romantic. It wasn't sexual. It wasn't "needy." It was more like a primal pull, a "knowing and being known" kind of drawing. From within her arose a conviction that here she faced a defining

moment, an opportunity to somehow be better than she'd ever imagined she could be.

The room was thick with aromas from the meal, smoke from the grilled lamb rising in tendrils toward the ceiling. Conversation buzzed about her, punctuated by laughter and accompanied by background music.

Clutching the present she had prepared, she wound her way through the group that had gathered around him, approaching with confidence but not without concern. When she reached him, he looked up at her and smiled. The crowd shifted to make room for her but then drew in a collective breath as she presented the beautiful flask, a work of art in itself.

Without hesitation, she snapped the long neck off the vessel, and richly perfumed oil bubbled from the opening, dripping onto her hands. Then she raised the bottle and extravagantly tipped its contents fully on his hair. The fragrant potion oozed down his temples, his cheeks, and onto his neck. Lifting his gaze, he met her eyes and received her offering with gratitude.

A hollow silence, awkward and stiff, descended on the room. One from his inner circle of friends barked out an objection: "What a waste! Think how many hungry people could have been fed with what it cost!" His words gave permission to the other stunned observers so that murmurs of disapproval traveled through the room. Rejection and judgment rained down on her.

Again he met her eyes, understanding the meaning of her gesture better than anyone else present. "She has done a beautiful thing. Yes, her gift was expensive, but the money that went for it would never pay for the food needed for all the hungry in the world. She meant this as an offering uniquely for me, to prepare me for what I am facing. She did what she could. And because she did what she could, what she did will be remembered as long as I am remembered."

Everyone's Story

Jesus said that because "she did what she could," her action would be remembered as long as he was remembered. She Did What She Could. S-D-W-S-C.

How many times had I read this story, heard it taught, or sat through a sermon about it and missed that sentence? I remembered the woman and her discomfort, her exposure. I remembered Jesus and his love for her. The perfume and its expense. The critical disciples and their judgmental comments. But this sentence—"She did what she could"—how had I missed it so many times?

As I read and reread it, I began to see Jesus' response to the woman in a way I hadn't before. He had defended the woman's action and pronounced that it would be paired with the Good News wherever it is preached throughout the world. It was so worthy, so accepted, so descriptive of God's love, that what she did would be permanently—eternally—attached to the Good News of God's gracious care for humanity.

Where else in Scripture is such a statement made? What was this beautiful thing that Jesus paired with the gospel? What did she do?

She did what she could.

Those five words hit me—hard. Rising up inside me and standing my heart at attention, they grabbed me and pushed me to a permanent paradigm shift.

She did what she could—SDWSC.

Whether it was related to the special needs adults in Serbia, the ravaged Congolese women, the children enslaved by sex traffickers, the AIDS orphans, the starving millions, or any other seemingly unfixable need before me, I had caught a glimpse of a life-shaping concept in this story about a woman who did what she could.

I lifted the corner of this thought to discover a fuller, broader, more challenging, and yet more realistic question than I'd ever considered before. A question that promised an answer within my grasp, not beyond it.

What if?

She did what she could. What if I did what I could? And you did what you could? So that we did what we could? Not necessarily in the Congo or in Serbia, but right here, right now, wherever God has planted each of us—all of us?

What if?

PART 1

She Did What She Could

She did what she could.
    She was a girl.
    God chose a girl to act.
    God chose a girl to change the world.

1
She Did What She Could

God chose a girl.

Mary of Bethany. We know her from Scripture as the sister of hardworking, hospitable Martha, in Luke 10, and of "up from the grave" Lazarus in John 11. The setting is their home in Bethany, about one and a half miles from Jerusalem.

The event takes place just days before Jesus' Triumphal Entry into Jerusalem, where he was hailed as King, fanned with palm branches, and celebrated as Messiah, and a little more than a week before his death for the sins of all humankind:

> Jesus was in Bethany at the home of Simon, a man who had previously had leprosy. While he was eating, a woman came in with a beautiful alabaster jar of

expensive perfume made from essence of nard. She broke open the jar and poured the perfume over his head.

Some of those at the table were indignant. "Why waste such expensive perfume?" they asked. "It could have been sold for a year's wages and the money given to the poor!" So they scolded her harshly.

But Jesus replied, "Leave her alone. Why criticize her for doing such a good thing to me? You will always have the poor among you, and you can help them whenever you want to. But you will not always have me. She did what she could and has anointed my body for burial ahead of time. I tell you the truth, wherever the Good News is preached throughout the world, this woman's deed will be remembered and discussed." (Mark 14:3-9)

Though Simon could have been just another follower of Jesus, he is more likely the elderly—and healed—father of Mary, Martha, and Lazarus. According to John 12, the criticizing voice comes from Judas Iscariot, who, known to have been greedy and a thief, helped himself to what was in the disciples' money bag. Other references indicate that some of the disciples were critical of the extravagance of Mary's act.

Although the story is told from different perspectives and gives different details, depending on which Gospel account you read, one important detail remains the same: Here, at this juncture in human history, God chose a *girl* to pair with the preaching of the Good News for all time to come.

Do you realize what a *big* deal this is?

We expect God to use men. He has chosen men

historically and purposefully. Men to prophesy. Men to rule. Men to lead. Men to follow a star across the wide world in search of the Christ child. Men to fish for other men. Men to form the church. Men to preach in the streets of early Christianity. The Bible is jam-packed with narratives and biographies and psalms of men, punctuated by an occasional female rendition.

That's fine. It's good—no—it's *great*! Humankind has much to learn from men. Men are *essential* to the expression of God's image in our world and to his purpose for the planet. And to be really clear—just because God chose a woman for this particular story doesn't mean that he *didn't* choose men to live out the message of this passage. As you read on in this little book, you'll increasingly understand how the point of the passage is that we—any of us—can change our world when we finally "get" how much we are loved in a relationship with God. God's love changes us. Radically. All of us. And when *we* are different, we make a difference in our world.

But *oh* how refreshing it is to hear a story sung in soprano! How healing and hopeful to see the curve of our own reflection in the turn of a tale. How much easier to understand a message spoken in our "first language." Sans translation. Often, women have to interpret stories, teachings, and illustrations from male to female—in church, in business, and in life. Such "bilingualism" is part of our everyday lives. But not here. Not this time. This story is first-person-female. The main character is a girl. A heroine. A *she*.

God chose a girl. A woman. A sitter at Jesus' feet, in contrast to a dissenter who betrayed him. And he paired her with the telling of the gospel for all time to come. Jesus said, "I tell you the truth, wherever the Good News is preached throughout the world, this woman's deed will be remembered and discussed" (Mark 14:9). God chose a woman who acted on her love for him in response to his love for her.

If this grabs your attention today, just imagine how God's choice sat with the crowd just after the crossroads of time between BC and AD, when women were little more than property. Slaves. Chattel. In fact, tradition held that each morning, Jewish males offered a blessing that thanked God for not making them Gentiles, slaves, or women.

The fact that Jesus invited women to accompany him on his journeys around Israel was shocking in itself. But to actually receive his livelihood off their generosity, to include them in his teaching, to equip them to serve and share in his post-Resurrection Kingdom work—that was *radical*. That he paired a girl and her gesture of love with the telling of the gospel for all time forward—such a choice slid beyond the comprehension of those present then—or even of many people now, for that matter.

But *God chose a girl*. Mary. We know her from passages contained in several of the Gospels. The apostle John seemed closest to her, as he included her most often in his chronicles of Christ. She chose to sit at Jesus' feet and learn from him rather than scurry about preparing food for him and others, as did her sister, Martha. Of course, there's nothing wrong with cooking. It's just that Mary innately desired the connection of communication, of learning, of presence.

In receiving the relationship Jesus offered her, she

discovered access to a faith-filled kind of living, one that tee-
tered between blind hope in some moments and tangible
returns on her trust in others. She saw her brother, Lazarus,
become ill, and she wailed for Jesus to journey to him and heal
him. She knew he could. When he did not, she stood, waiting to learn from him yet again. Having already seen Lazarus's lifeless body sealed in a tomb, she watched Jesus weep
at the loss of her kin—his friend—and absorbed in her soul
how very much he truly cared. And then, stunningly, unexpectedly, beyond her comprehension, she witnessed the miracle of Lazarus alive before her, clearly breathing, although his
grave clothes were still intact. She would likely remember this
moment later, on a bright morning at sunrise, outside another
tomb.

God chose a girl. He had certainly called women forward to his Kingdom purposes before. Through Eve, life was
born into the world. In Deborah, justice reigned over Israel.
Through Bathsheba, a great king was brought forth. Rahab
served to save God's people, as did Esther. Mary birthed God's
son. Tabitha (Dorcas) and Priscilla carried forward efforts in
the early church. And Mary, this Mary of Bethany, was paired
with the gospel forever.

God chose a girl. A woman. Like me. Like you. Like your
coworker or your subordinate or your boss. Like your neighbor
or your child's best friend. Like your mother or your sister or
your daughter or your aunt or your niece or your granddaugh-
ter. God chose a girl to pair with the gospel forever. Look over
your shoulder at her. Look in the mirror at her. Elevate her

voice, her heart, her actions to the Kingdom possibilities they contain.

God chose a girl—and *she* did what she could.

● ● ●

She'd adopted him as a baby. Dimpled, chunky, and beautiful, he thrilled at the sound of her voice, her smell. He'd been a challenge to raise. Bright, creative, unendingly energetic, he delighted in the smallest life moments: discovering a caterpillar humping along a sidewalk on a summer afternoon, careering his plastic Big Wheel down the driveway, swinging higher and higher and higher at the park.

As he grew into his tween and then teen years, his talent for sports emerged: a stunningly fast fifty-yard-dash time. He made friends easily but had not been able to keep them without her help. Schoolwork demanded an attention and focus he didn't possess without the help of medication. He finished high school, finally, and flitted from this to that, from waiting tables to construction to trade school, all the while roller-coastering his moods with drugs and alcohol.

He was arrested for drunk driving and released without much penalty. Again. And again. He did jail time.

She knew he was still drinking. And driving. A danger to himself and to those around him.

From across the country, she called the Virginia Highway Patrol and reported his license plate and his habit. They noted her concern in their state's database, leaving her completely unsure whether or not her "mother's plea" had made any difference.

But she did what she could.

*She **did** what she could.*
 She acted.
 She didn't just think about acting.
 She didn't act out of obligation.
 She didn't let others act for her.
 She didn't wait to be invited.

2
She **Did** What She Could

Mary didn't just think about doing something. She didn't pledge to herself, *I'll do something sometime*, feel better in that moment, and then forget about it.

She didn't "take her turn" out of obligation. Or because she had to. Because it was the festival season and doing nice things was expected, even required.

She didn't vicariously invest through the gestures of others. Observing from a safe distance as other people invested would have been much easier. Less obvious. More expected. Far less risky.

She didn't wait to be invited. If she had, there would have been little question of the appropriateness of her action. Then the response of others in the room wouldn't have been her fault.

But if she thought and didn't act, she would regret not

offering the comfort she longed to give. If she had taken her turn out of obligation, the action would have lacked meaning. If she had stood as an observer rather than engage as a participant, she would not have experienced the personal satisfaction of involvement. If she had waited to be invited, she might never have moved, for she might not have been invited in the *expected* sense of the word.

Pushing past the paralysis that might have kept her body still, moving despite the objections in her head and the hesitations in her heart, she acted.

There was a *nowness* to her action. Recognizing that she was living in a moment that might never be repeated, she acted. Right then. When it would matter most to Jesus, she ministered to his body *before* his death. She seized the moment, knowing it was hers to invest.

What courage! What tenacity! Yes. There was that. For a woman to act with such abandon was truly bold in those days.

There was also a *naturalness* to her action. The verb tense used in the original language is one that describes a real event that actually transpired. This was an everyday action. Mary simply put her passion into play and did what she could.

She acted out of her love. She knew that Jesus loved her, and she loved him back. She *lived* loved. That's the whole point of the gospel, isn't it? Jesus' death on the cross giving humankind access to the one perfect God, who cannot tolerate imperfection or even unintended failure. The gospel is grace given to all in need of it so that they can—finally—return love to the Creator. Their Creator.

She *did* what she could. A verb. An action. Moving and implementing her love in a way that mattered, she *did*.

● ● ●

It had been a busy morning, even more so than usual. She'd dropped the boys at day care, her eldest now in a "hanging back" stage so that she'd nearly had to pry him off her leg as she left. As she headed to the office, she realized she was hungry and pulled into the drive-through. She merged quickly in front of another car, lowered her window, and ordered a breakfast burrito and a large Coke. Then, as she pulled forward, it hit her: She hadn't just *merged* in front of the sedan behind her; she had cut in front of it.

Oh my gosh! No wonder the other driver had glared at her—and gestured not too nicely. Even though she'd had a trying morning, she felt rotten. Sure, she might not ever see this person again, but it didn't seem right to just ignore her blunder.

Then the solution registered. She handed a five-dollar bill through her window and instructed the attendant to put the money toward the order of the driver behind her. There. Better. She pulled forward and watched in her rearview mirror as the driver leaned toward the window with an astonished expression and then turned forward with a smile.

Yes, better indeed. She did what she could.

*She did **what** she could.*
  She acted out of what she had, not
    what she wished she had.
  *She did **what** she could, not all she*
    could.

3
She Did **What** She Could

The "what" Mary chose is significant.

In parallel tellings of the story, her siblings chose their roles in the room. Her sister, Martha, served—a role familiar but reframed after Jesus' first visit to their home, when she had lost herself in the preparations and had missed out on Jesus' presence. Their resurrected and restored brother, Lazarus, reclined at the table, a symbolic centerpiece of what lay ahead for Jesus. Mary could again sit attentively at Jesus' feet—in the past, Jesus had praised her for choosing the "one thing worth being concerned about" (Luke 10:42)—or she could choose another role.

The "what" she chose shaped her role.

Picture her considering her options. She mentally sorts through her various skills: Could she dance or sing or recite something from the Hebrew Scriptures? Her thoughts pivot to her possessions, few truly valuable ones among them: her brush or her robe or a pot she had formed?

So not enough. None of it appropriate. If only she had more to choose from . . . something unique, expensive, worthy. She closed down her thoughts against the rationalization of what she didn't have and surveyed—honestly and carefully— what she did have. Then, from all the "whats" she possessed, she chose one specific "what" for the moment.

The flask of nard. *Yes,* she thought.

Nard was made from the aromatic oil extracted from the root of a nard plant, likely grown in India. A rose-red substance known as spikenard, it would have been the Chanel No. 5 of its day. Its going rate was three hundred denarii, which was equivalent to about a year's salary. Such a valuable essence was transported in a decorative flask or a box that was, in itself, a valuable work of art. Sometimes shaped like a flower or a rosebud, the alabaster or marble flask had a long neck and was actually sealed in such a way that the neck of the bottle had to be broken in order to access the perfume. Once it had been broken, there was no way to close it again— no cork, no lid, no stopper. Whatever wasn't used in the first application ended up wasted.[1]

A smile grew in Mary's heart as she settled on this particular gift to express her love for Jesus. It was a lavish gift. One that she herself likely had received from the hand of another and had saved, treasured, even, not wanting to open and enjoy it, since in doing so she would also spend the comfort of its promise.

She settled on her "what" and gave it without looking

back. There were no regrets. No *buts*. Just giving. Not from
what she didn't have but from the one thing she had that
would truly make a difference, speak her love, meet the need,
compassionately connect to Jesus as he was facing what would
no doubt be the most challenging moment of his life on earth.

Oh, and lest we send ourselves over the edge of self-sacri-
fice here, note that she did *what* she could. Not *all* she could.

Rather than give this—and that—and then some more,
only to eventually fall, spent, at his feet, she gave what she
could and left it at that. Enough. A lot. Just right. She chose
what she could—and gave it ungrudgingly.

● ● ●

He noticed the cars lining the street, many more than normal. They
streamed out of one driveway: his neighbors', two doors down. The
one with the live-in elderly grandfather.

He must have passed away, he thought.

He sat on the bench on his porch, facing the house, and
watched as folks flapped out the screen door and made their way to
their cars, sputtered the engines, and drove up the street. A woman
arrived in a minivan, hobbled around to the sliding door to with-
draw a casserole, and then trudged up the steps. Children tumbled
about on the lawn. A delivery person brought a flower arrangement.

He thought through his options. Not much of a cook, he had
no food to prepare. Uncomfortable with caring for children, he
turned away and stared thoughtfully into the air before him.

Then he rose and ducked into his own front door, made his
way to his bedroom closet, and pulled down a wooden box from

the top shelf. Tucking it under his arm, he headed back out, down his steps, and across the patchy grass between his home and his neighbors'. Up the steps, to the screen door. He looked inside at the small crowd chatting amiably, and met the eyes of the old man's daughter.

"I came to shine the shoes," he said.

"Shoes?" she asked with raised eyebrows.

"Yes, shoes. For the service. It's what I can do."

The woman smiled and opened the door wide, allowing him—with his wooden box of polish and brushes—to enter.

Following her to the kitchen, he waited while she made a quick trip through the house. Then, he settled down to shine the shoes. He did what he could.

*She did what **she** could.*
She was a specific woman with a specific story who acted out of the particulars of her life.
She acted because she knew she was loved and wanted to love back.

4
*She Did What **She** Could*

Before we go any further, let's be clear about who "she" was. It's easy to get confused here. Because this story is told in three of the four gospels—Matthew (26:6-13), Mark (14:3-9), and John (12:1-8)—we sometimes assume that a similar story told in Luke 7:36-50 is the same story. But it's not. It's not the same people or the same setting, it didn't take place at the same time, and it doesn't have the same message. That's a shadow story about another woman who anointed Jesus.

Let's dive a little deeper.

Both stories take place in the home of a man named Simon. But our story occurs in the home of Simon the Leper (likely the once infirm and now healed father of Mary, Martha, and Lazarus), and Luke's story is about Simon the Pharisee.

In both stories, the central character is a woman. But

our story's heroine is Mary of Bethany, a good friend and follower of Jesus who knew him so well that she understood his impending death and the significance of her gesture of preburial anointing. Luke's story is of an "immoral," (some translations say "sinful") woman. We're never told her name. And though we're all "sinful," the underlying meaning of Luke's description refers to her reputation in the town—likely for prostitution. Mary of Bethany was not a prostitute. The sinful woman was not Mary Magdalene, either. Mary Magdalene was a woman from whom Jesus had cast out demons and who then became a follower (Luke 8:2).

Both stories depict a woman anointing Jesus with expensive perfume. We don't know where Mary of Bethany might have received the nard, but a prostitute could easily have been paid in perfume for her services and thus had it handy to bring forward to Jesus in the story in Luke.

Both stories describe the woman pouring the perfume on Jesus—sometimes on his head, sometimes on his feet. Anointing a guest with oil was customary in that culture, though usually with just a few drops on the head. In two of the three Gospels (Matthew and Mark), Mary of Bethany anoints Jesus' head. In John's Gospel, she pours the oil on his feet. Scholars suggest that this head-to-toe gesture made sense as people reclined at the table while dining in New Testament times. It also symbolized Mary's preparing Jesus' body for burial.

In Luke, the "sinful" woman washed Jesus' feet—a task usually performed by a slave or servant at the host's direction. In Jesus' remarks about the woman's gesture, he points out that he'd been denied this normal practice of hospitality prior to her effort. When she dried his feet with her loosened hair, the crowd was aghast, because a woman's unbound hair evidenced her loose-woman status and was socially inappropriate. Way too intimate for such a public gathering, perhaps the equivalent of greeting a stranger with a French kiss. But the woman's action resulted from her gratitude for Jesus' touch on her heart, a motivation he understood and received as she intended. (In a way, *this* woman also did what she could. . . .) In John's gospel, Mary of Bethany also wiped Jesus' feet with her loosened hair, but not because it was her habit to be provocative. Rather, she did so out of her relationship of spiritual intimacy.

So there we are: four Gospels, two Simons, two women, two jars of perfume, one Mary, one Jesus—and two separate stories.

Now let's get back to ours.

Mary of Bethany did what *she* could. She gave from the context of who God had made her to be—and from what her relationship with him was making her. She sat at Jesus' feet, opening her soul to his teaching, his wisdom, and his love. Because she took the time to take him in, she "got" him. Over the days and months and, perhaps, years of their relationship, his investment combined with the core of her being to yield a rich essence of character, from which she later anointed him in a moment of his own great need. Spiritual intimacy had been formed, and in return, it formed her.

Because she had received love, she gave it. She understood what, so far, the disciples had missed. In this act of worship, she *lived* loved.

Mary approached Jesus with her gift of perfume and poured it out with confidence, her gesture expressing her love for him and preparing his body for burial before his death, the broken flask foreshadowing the shards customarily left in the tomb after the body's anointing for burial.[1]

Her gift touched Jesus in the moment, the fragrant oil running off his hair, down his temples and onto his neck and his chest, comforting him with love when it mattered most to him.

I wonder whether later, Mary's gift gave again: as Jesus prayed in a midnight garden setting, tortured by thoughts of what lay ahead and privately battling with his destiny. As he stood before the high priest, and then Pilate, then Herod, and then back before Pilate, enduring their ridicule and accusations. As the thorny crown was smashed down on his head. As he bent his back under the lashes of the whips. As he struggled to carry a heavy cross through the streets of Jerusalem and up a dusty hill. As he was laid out on that cross and fixed to it by heavy iron nails through his hands and feet. And as he hung in crucifixion.

As his head fell to his chest, dipping under the weight of his suffering, did any fragrance still linger, mingling with the stench of blood, and bring back, however briefly, that tender moment? In those hours of torture, when the soldiers taunted him by shaking wine before his parched lips, did the remembrance of her gift revive his soul? As he turned to the right and the left, taking in the two suffering with him and offering to each of them the hope of heaven, did any remaining fragrance convince his frail humanity of the truth of his own promise? As he looked down and beseeched his dear friend and follower John to take in his mother as his own and to care for her after his death, did any small part of the smell rise from his chest to his nostrils and warm him with comfort that, indeed, she would be held close in her grief?

Jesus gave Mary of Bethany access to himself. Because she had fully received all he'd held out to her in his presence and his teaching and his very being, she had been forever changed. She acted from the reality of the relationship she shared with him.

To Jesus, Mary gave a gift that kept on giving. She did what *she* could. She let him love her.

● ● ●

She slid into the booth, set her purse beside her, and took up the menu. It had been a good morning. Her idea had found favor with her boss. Likely there was a bit of a bonus in the works.

Within a few minutes she was joined by her lunch date. As they exchanged greetings, the waitress approached, slapped down two waters and then paused, jutting out a hip and requesting their drink order.

Something about their server drew her attention. Her hair stuck out in spikes from some kind of amassment atop her head, its brassy-blonde color contrasting to her salon-tanned skin. Thick eyeliner. Long fake nails. A smoker's voice. Hollow, pain-filled eyes.

After giving her drink and food order, she fell into familiar conversation with her friend, and the time passed quickly until the waitress returned to present the check. Plopping it down, she heeled and walked away, revealing a tear in her skirt and, further down, a hole in her black, gum-soled shoe.

After splitting the check with her friend, she scanned down the receipt to *Gratuity*, poised her pen, paused, poised it again, paused again, and then wrote in an amount equal to the check's total. She signed her name, flipped the folder shut, and sat back, oddly surprised but peaceful. No, she couldn't pay that much for a meal *every* day. After all, that bonus might never come. But today, she could. So, she did what *she* could.

*She did what she **could**.*
    She acted with what she had.
    She acted where she was.
    She acted when it mattered.

5
She Did What She **Could**

Mary grabbed hold of what she possessed—what was within her reach, under her power, obedient to her control—and she invested it. She did what she could with what she had to work with. She took the bottle of nard and made the most of it, right then and there.

Now, surely, she had other options from which to choose. Less valuable, less—well—less *extravagant*. This gesture was a little like wearing sequins to a picnic or pulling out the Dom Pérignon for a potluck. Mary gave to Jesus what was likely her most valuable asset—her pension. Her insurance. Her equity. Her savings. She gave up her goods to give Jesus what she could in a moment of significance and meaning unlike any other in his life or in hers. *Wow*. She could have *way* overdone here.

But as we've already stated, while the nard was expensive

and extravagant, it was *specifically* the right gift for this pre-death moment. When we look at the other elements in Mary's "could," her follow-through makes even more sense.

She acted with what she had—*where she was*. For Mary, this meant acting in public. Perhaps the thought had occurred to her in private as she prepared for the dinner, applying a dab of her "everyday" perfume to her neck. But it had then moved with her out into the group gathered for the meal, out into the open for all to see—and evaluate.

She could have played it safe, holding the gift until a more private moment, a less risky spot, free from scrutiny. But, no, she pulled out all the stops and plunged ahead into an act that would forever commit her to Christ as her motivation for living. Symbolically baptizing her soul before a room of observers, she gave testimony of her changed life. Marrying her heart to him, she vowed her loyalty, faithfulness, and commitment.

She acted with what she had: She acted where she was, and she acted when it mattered. She acted purposefully.

Was it a calculated moment? Had she preplanned the "sermon" she was about to offer? Probably not. In fact, a sermon of any kind was a very unlikely offering for her, the seemingly quiet sort. Yet her expression of commitment to Christ invited others to decide what they would do with him. Her action forced the hands of all present, moving them to either relationship or rejection. Who did they think Jesus was? Did they grasp what was at stake? Would they believe? Would they follow? Would they let him love them?

Judas led the rejection, accusing Mary of frivolous waste

during a Passover celebration at which, traditionally, gifts were given to the poor, not to each other. He had a point. Mary could have sold the perfume at a huge profit—enough to live on for a year—and then she could have given that entire amount to the poor. In fact, during this celebration season, such an action would have been valued and deemed highly appropriate. Righteous, even.

Yes, she could have loved Jesus by serving the poor. But she knew there would be other opportunities for that. In this week, on this night, the most compelling expression of her love for Jesus was to act in response to his love for her: To lavishly love him back in a tangible, lingering endowment would mean the most in this precise moment and then would help carry him through his suffering for her and for all humankind.

She recognized the juncture before her, chose her path of devotion to Jesus, and by her gesture, invited others to follow. An evangelist for living loved, she gave an "altar call" for all present to do the same—to demonstrate their commitment to being Christ followers by doing what they could. Her deed became paired with the gospel because it spelled out *how* to follow in everyday action.

She acted with what she had. She acted where she was. She acted when it mattered.

She did what she *could*.

● ● ●

She had served as a leader in the nonprofit effort for more than three years. Her heart had been twisted this way and that as she slugged her way through challenge after challenge, and her reward was the tangible growth of the staff she led. Of those involved in her ministry, 97 percent reported that they had grown in their faith. That was satisfying. *Deeply* satisfying.

But the troubled economy squeezed hard on the organization. Donations decreased to less than 60 percent of budget. Salaries were slashed. After months of trying every other option, she saw the dreaded words *reduction of workforce* on the memo handed down from the board of directors.

The memo contained a list with two headings: "Remaining Staff" and "Released Staff." She read the names on each, haunted as she saw her own suggestions appearing in one column or the other. As her eyes moved down the names of those to be laid off, she absorbed the reality of one name in particular and swallowed hard. *Shannon.* Hired only a few months ago, the newly married, pregnant young woman had recently been evicted and would need help to land on her feet after yet another setback.

She reached for her wallet, grateful that she'd been to the ATM the day before. But as she counted out the cash, she thought twice. It wasn't enough. She considered her own diminished salary and the needs of her own family. Then she reached for her checkbook.

She did what she could.

As a result of her action . . . she was
  ridiculed.
  As a result of her action . . . she was
    honored.

The relationship resulted in a response.

6
She Did What She Could

As a result of her action, she was . . . ridiculed.

Judas, Jesus' eventual betrayer, aims the first spear of criticism at Mary's gift. As if emboldened by his example, others join in, creating a clattering of verbal strikes fired at Mary's bent frame: *What a ridiculous waste! Completely unnecessary! So inappropriate! Outrageous! How embarrassing! Who does she think she is? She needs to get herself together! Someone do something! Stop it! Stop it now!*

Many socially minded sorts today might agree about the apparent waste of what would easily have provided a year's groceries for an average family. Moralists of our time might wince at the squandering of the lavish, designer-label offering when its value could have accomplished so much good. Reputable nonprofit organizations leverage such amounts every day for the maximum benefit. Any good financial manager could have come up with a smarter use for the funds.

Imagine Mary chewing her lip in concern as she reconsidered her gesture and the resulting ridicule.

But Jesus' response? "Leave her alone." A command. Instead of telling *her* to stop, he orders that *they* cease their abuse—their blaming, sighing, enraged criticizing—of her.

"Why criticize her for doing such a good thing to me?" he asks in Mark 14:6. Instead of wondering about her action, he questions their intrusion into a sacred moment of ministry. Their paining, troubling, wearying of her—and him—in contrast to her comforting of him. Their heads, full of picky, irrelevant debate, in contrast to her heart, full of love.

As for the "waste" of the perfume in a time when the poor could have benefited from the investment, Jesus compared the poor—who would always be around and whom they could help whenever they wanted—with his own temporary earthly presence. What is ever wasted when it is invested at the only possible time—today?

As a result of her action . . . she was honored.

Look into Judas's face the way Jesus might have seen it, and you wonder at his gall. He was willing to sell out the one he should have seen as his King for thirty silver coins—about 120 days' wages—whereas Mary blessed the Lord she loved with a gift worth closer to a year's salary. Judas, who as "treasurer" held the responsibility of stewarding the money for the movement, could have—maybe should have—initiated a customary outpouring to the underserved during this feast time. Who really loved the poor more?

Jesus pronounces Mary's action "a good thing." Literally, he defines it a "noble" thing. The perfect thing to do in the moment. Mary knew that she was loved, and she responded to God's embrace by loving him back—right then, when he needed it and could receive it. *She did what she could.*

Jesus pairs her action with the telling of the gospel from that time forth. On the surface, this seems an odd pairing: A girl, and the gospel? A lavish outpouring of oil, and salvation? In the umpteen times you may have heard the story of Jesus, of his life, death, and resurrection, how often have you heard Mary's gesture included?

Both Matthew and Mark include this pronouncement. Could they simply have meant every time *their* Gospels were proclaimed, her act would be included? Maybe. But what if they meant that *Jesus* was making this pairing? What might Jesus have meant? Perhaps he meant that every time the gospel—the Good News of present help and eternal hope through Jesus' death on the cross for our sins—is proclaimed, it will be paired with the radical reality of Mary's relationship with Jesus, the kind of relationship that we, too, can enjoy. Jesus paired the gospel with a relationship of love that expresses itself in loving service. Salvation is not fire insurance, a ticket to heaven, a transaction to eternal life. Salvation is being transformed by a relationship of love.

Jesus paired Mary's loving act with the gospel for all time because, plain and simple, the gospel is love lived out.

She did what she could when she could. And because she did, she was ridiculed—and honored. So, now what? Exactly. Now . . . what?

If she did what she could—when she could—what difference would it make if I did what I could? How might what I could do connect to the expression of hope and love available in Jesus for others to see, to grab hold of, to integrate into their beings and doings?

What if *I* did what I could?

PART 2

What If
I Did
What I
Could?

What if . . .
   I *did what I could?*
   I'm a girl.
   What would it mean for me to act?
   What if I could change the world?

7
What If . . .
I *Did What I Could?*

What if *I* acted? I'm a woman whom God loves. What if I just start there: I am loved.

I used to think such a thing was silly, immature, unnecessary. Unworthy me? Loved by God? Humph! Shame would gurgle up in my soul against such a thought. In seconds, a "shame fest" would overtake me, quietly and in secret, and I felt like a child caught in a naughty act.

Mary's action shifts me away from that shame. It's not that I deserve to be loved. I don't. She didn't. No one really does. It's just that Jesus loves me. It's a fact. When I realize that I'm not so darling in and of myself and that I don't have to be—but that I am still irrevocably loved and valued and created for good—in such moments his love becomes all the more stunning to me.

What if *I* did what I could?

Wait—me? I'm just a girl. Exactly. In Mary, God chose a girl. I like describing her this way. A girl. It seems so much more doable than saying God chose a *woman*. Somehow, I can't relate to that word. When I hear the word *woman*, suddenly the effort feels too big, too responsible, and too hard for me. Issues of what it means to be a grown-up *woman* weigh down my shoulders. The littleness in me squirms in discomfort at the idea of this pressurized role. Childhood worries and inadequacies whirl around me. I go all prepubescent. Before I can even inventory my offerings, when I hear *woman*—I'm done.

So I start with *girl*. I can *be* a girl. I *am* a girl. A female in the process of growing into the world of the word *woman*. I can be that.

God chose a girl. God chose me. To do what *I* could. So what could *I* do? Let me think: *I* am middle-aged. *I* am a wife. *I* am a mother. *I* am a grandmother. *I* run a nonprofit ministry organization. *I* can write and speak and make awesome mashed potatoes. *I* am the child of divorced parents and the product of a home riddled with alcohol abuse. *I* carry with me emotional bruises from intangible wounds, and *I* also have experienced great healing and power over these afflictions.

I am creative. An original kind of thinker. An effusive leader. A passionate strategist. An energetic visionary. There are some pretty good things there. But what about the other parts of me?

I am impatient, controlling, and judgmental at times. *I* can be insecure and disrespectful. *I* am selfish. Sometimes insincere, know-it-all-ish, and shortsighted.

Doing what *I* could means bringing me, all of me, to the realization that I am loved by God and that from that love, *I* can act. The good, fun parts of me and the not-so-great parts of me too.

What if *I* did what I could?

I grew up in Houston, Texas. My days started with the sound of my mother's alarm clock blaring from way down the hall in our ranch-style home. I pushed back my covers and padded into the kitchen, where I found a glass, filled it with ice cubes, and poured Coke to the top. I grabbed a couple of chocolate chip cookies and made my way back down the hall to my mother's room, where I set this "breakfast" on her nightstand, turned off the alarm, and began the process of trying to shake her awake.

I was ten or eleven years old. My mother and father had divorced when I was five. My mother had lost herself in alcohol, and it had become my job to get her up and off to work in the morning.

For years, I mothered my mother and yearned for the very occasional visit from my father. My mother tried to mother us. She created Christmas celebrations filled with magic and fun that blearily faded into the topaz glow of Scotch as Christmas Day culminated. She did what she could to offer us a home and a hope for our lives.

I was by no means a perfect daughter—but I was a good one. There were times when I did what I could for my mother: waking her up in the morning, watching over my younger brother when she was unpredictable, cooking dinner when she was unable to do so. There were other times when what

I could do really meant *not* doing something: not letting my mother's instability prohibit my choice to leave and begin my own life. Not being "nice" but rather allowing some distance to grow between us in order for me to find my way out of code-pendency. Not accepting whatever she gave but instead insisting on certain boundaries in how she handled herself in my home when she visited my children, her grandchildren.

I know that though I am scarred in some ways, my offerings have been formed out of the very "me-ness" of my upbringing. My mother's illness shaped my resilience. I am who I am, with my strengths and my deficits, because of her—both her strengths and her deficits.

While I'm "better," healed of much, I am still being shaped. All that hangs back as unworthy in me finds the hope of healing that comes in a relationship with Jesus. All of me is welcomed by all of him.

What if . . . from the reality of who I am and who I have become—all of it—*I* did what I could? The question is unsettling—prodding, annoying, challenging—and then, somehow, freeing.

And you? What would it mean for *you* to do what *you* could?

No, you're not all you want to be, nor are you some superstar. You're *you*—okay in some areas and not in others. You, with the polka-dot track record of efforts, some successful, others not so much. You, with the great intentions and the occasional follow-through. You, with the past. You, with the present. You, with the commitments that stretch into the future. What about you?

Think about David—with deep potholes of adultery and murder behind him—looking at the road ahead and wondering how God could use him. Peter—Mr. Denial in the moment when Jesus could have used a good word—reinstated to be the earthly head of the church. Rahab—used just as she was, prostitute status and all—to save the spies of Israel.

Or Mary. Just a girl whom God chose to pair with the gospel because she did what she could.

Or me. A once-upon-a-time-girl-now-middle-aged-woman whom God tapped to train, to marry, to mother, to lead, to speak, to write, to love, to listen, to learn.

● ● ●

Sometimes it's in everyday situations, when I'm taking out the trash and notice the neighbors' sprinkler is overflowing into the street. So I go knock on their door and tell them. Sometimes it's in heroic surprise as my feet run to the side of a swimming pool and I lunge into the water to pull a toddler back to the surface, all under the glazed-over gaze of a lifeguard who missed it. Sometimes in a stunning moment I realize *I'm* the one to apologize to my husband for making a rude comment, or leave work to rescue my sick grandson at daycare, or stand up and speak at a meeting.

Me.

What if *you and I* did what we could—because we are loved?

*What if . . . I **did** what I could?*
   What if I acted?
   What if I didn't just think about acting
      but actually acted?
   What if I didn't act out of obligation?
   What if I didn't let others act for me?
   What if I didn't wait to be invited?
   What if I didn't just wonder about
      what difference I could make but
      actually took a step?

8
What If . . .
I **Did** What I Could?

I'm standing in the shower and thinking of calling a couple that has been through a tough time with their kids. I know it would mean a lot to them. I don't have solutions to their problems, but I know from my own experience that the companionship of someone who has "been there" is still meaningful. I decide to invite them to come for dinner. I don't plan to pronounce a solution over their world; I know I can't. But we can listen, my husband and I.

As I lather my hair, I think through my schedule and mentally select a few dates to double-check. I even get as far as planning a menu. There. Good.

I exit the shower, dress, and leave for my day. I check off meetings and tasks and other items on my to-do list. I drive home. The evening passes. Another day. And another. And I don't call.

Why? No real reason. The whole matter leaves the front of my mind, and I kind of forget about it—until I run into the mom unexpectedly and I feel my face redden at the reminder of my inaction. Does she notice? I ratchet up the compassion in my face and ask some specific questions about her daughter to prove that I really have been engaged in what she's going through, even though I've done nothing to demonstrate my concern.

I decide too much time has passed to act now. It would be awkward. When the faces of these family members appear in my mind, I pray for them. I wonder how the whole thing is progressing—and still I don't act.

But what if I *did* what I could?

What if I didn't just think about it; what if I actually *acted*? I'm not talking about "fixing" her daughter or curing her son. I'm just talking about doing what I could. Fix a meal. Give her a hug. That would be something. It would likely be enough.

I have lots of great ideas that I never follow through on. But what if I did?

What if I didn't just do what I was obligated to do but actually invested and did something that I knew would matter? Like planning my day so that when I attend an event, I can stay for the whole thing rather than just dash in and out to make an appearance. Like hanging out at church before or after the service in order to connect with people who could use some friendship. Like listening for the real response beneath the "fine" I receive when I ask a coworker how he's doing.

What if I didn't take the easy road of allowing everyone else around me to invest? What if I didn't excuse my own lack of action with the rationalization that what I could have done and didn't was really unnecessary, repetitive, or unvalued anyway? *They have enough canned food. Nobody will notice if I don't volunteer in my child's class this year. My twenty-five dollars won't make a dent.*

What if instead of waiting to be invited, I jumped in, took the initiative, volunteered, offered my two widow's mites?

As I look back at my life, I can trace a pattern of requests preceding nearly all my involvements: Would you serve on the committee? Would you give your money? Would you help? A call. A question. An invitation. I tended to conclude that initiating action on my own was, well, pushy, bossy, even arrogant. Who did I think I was?

But Mary wasn't "invited." Strictly speaking, Jesus never said, "Hey, Mary, would you please do something especially outstanding for me right now? Something I can hold up as an example for all time to come?"

God gives all of us skills, talents, gifts, possessions, personalities. He creates us to be and to do, and to braid our being into our doing and our doing into our being. I don't wait to be invited to "be." Why would I have to wait to be invited to "do"?

A friend meets my eyes and offers a challenge: "What can you do that no one has ever invited you to do?" I make a list. I am amazed at the variety of very doable tasks I tally. I can put colors together in a room or an outfit. I can use word pictures to describe feelings and situations in ways that communicate clearly. I can see where efforts are headed before they get there. I can identify forces motivating relationships and negotiate through them. Most days, nobody specifically asks me to invest these abilities. Does that mean I shouldn't bring them forward?

Perhaps I need to grab hold of the reality that what God has *equipped* me to do, he has *invited* me to do.

What if I moved beyond all these obstacles—thinking about acting but not acting, acting out of obligation, figuring someone else will act so I don't need to, and waiting to be invited in order to act? What if I actually took a step? What if . . . I *did* what I could?

What gap would be filled? What need would be met? What answer would be offered? What question would be asked?

Just recently another friend prodded me to stay in a selection process for a position I felt was out of my league.

"Why?" I pushed back. "I'm not a good fit. It's silly."

"Because," she said, "your presence in the process will help reveal who the right candidate is."

Hmm. I'd never considered that.

And you. What if you *did* what you could? What if you didn't just think about acting but actually followed through?

In our minds, we make it so hard, don't we? We think we have to *plan it out*. We have to *try harder*. In reality, there are opportunities all day, every day, right in front of us. Opportunities to just do what we could. Or maybe even to stop doing something in order to create space to do what we could.

Not convinced yet? Okay. What if you *didn't* do what you could? *Ugh*. Here comes the guilt. There are so very many "she *didn't* do what she could" stories, in my life—and in yours. They point the finger of accusation at us, and we squirm in discomfort.

● ● ●

She had been visiting a friend in the hospital, and as she walked toward the elevator, she felt the heaviness of all that lay ahead: more chemo, more family juggling, fewer resources to meet the need. She punched the down arrow, lifted her head, and focused on a man in a wheelchair to her left. He must have been in his sixties—maybe seventies. Clearly he was in pain as he hunched in his chair, his gnarled fingers combing his matted hair back from his brow, his mouth a grimace, his eyes slits.

Forgetting for a moment her own burden, she sensed a pull to go to him, to put her hand on his shoulder and utter a simple prayer of peace and healing over his soul.

Then, as if shrugging inwardly, she dismissed the tug she had felt. She was a stranger to this man. He would think her odd. The elevator doors opened, and she stepped inside. Adjusting the familiar mantle of her friend's illness about her shoulders, she selected her floor.

But like a photograph framed on a wall in her mind, the image of that man haunted her. Two days later she could still see him as clearly as she had in that moment at the elevator. And two months later, a vague grief continued to pull at her heart. *Why hadn't she obeyed the instinct?*

● ● ●

He was driving home from the office, in a hurry to make his daughter's homecoming dinner at the holidays. How he had missed her! Her first semester away at college had been planned with a measure of expectation that life at home would be different. But her launch out of the nest had torn a surprising hole in the fabric of his days.

The snow accumulating on his windshield made driving a challenge, but the road was familiar, and he felt a purposeful confidence moving him along. Then, through the snow, he saw something on the side of the road. In the twilight he made out a car—some no-brand, two-door model—with part of its body raised, like a dog hiking its leg. *Flat tire.*

He slowed to take in the details: two people, one clearly a young woman. And the other? Surely a man—yeah—that looked like a guy helping.

Speeding up again, he glanced in his rearview mirror and wondered. *Was* it a guy? It had been hard to tell in the swirling snow. Did they have a spare? Should he have stopped?

He thought about it all the way home. And later that night, after chili and coffee and catch-up conversation, he went to bed, still wondering if a girl like his daughter had made it to her destination after all, or if she'd been stranded in the snow.

Nobody's going to do life 100 percent perfectly all the time. There are plenty of moments when it makes good sense for us to punch the elevator button, descend to our cars, and go home after a grueling hospital visit. Plowing through a snowstorm to meet our newly returned, precious child is completely understandable. I don't think anyone expects you or me to do and do and do and do what can be done, just so we won't feel haunted or bugged or bad.

And it's not just regular folks like you and me who don't do what we can. The disciples didn't stay awake in the garden of Gethsemane with Jesus—as he'd asked them to. The Bible traces story after story of God's very messed-up people not doing what they could. Peter didn't admit he knew Jesus in the Temple square. John Mark didn't remain on Paul's second missionary journey but for some reason abandoned him. Moses didn't control his anger. David didn't resist his attraction to Bathsheba.

So welcome to the club. We all blow it. SDWSC is not about guilt avoidance. It's not about paying it forward or doing random acts of kindness or living a better life. It's not about obedience just for the sake of obedience.

If I *did* what I could, I would be acting out of God's love for me in a given moment when he has more for me to experience. More, because I move beyond considering to engaging. More, because I invest out of an attitude of caring rather than out of a sense of obligation. More, because I act instead of letting someone else act. More, because I initiate, knowing that because I *am*, I can *do*.

More, because I do instead of don't.

What if I *did* what I could?

What would it mean if I *did* what I could? What if you *did* too?

*What if . . . I did **what** I could?*

> *What if I quit focusing on what I don't have and considered instead what I do have?*

> *What if I let go of the pressure to do everything I could and instead did the one thing I could do now?*

> *What if I started right now, in this moment, in this season of life, to do what I could?*

9

What If . . .
I Did **What** *I Could?*

What? What could I possibly do that would make a difference today? Twenty-four million people die of starvation every day. I don't have a fancy jar of oil worth a year of my wages. What *do* I have? What is my "nard"?

I have a house, a car, an income, my health. But I need those things. What can I do when I don't think I have anything I don't need? Does God expect me to give the most expensive thing I have? My best stuff—and only my best stuff?

Let's look at the flip side: I'm exhausted, broke, scared, busy. What can I give out of what I *don't* have? More time? More effort? More trying? I'm too tired to think about more of anything. I don't have any "more."

In John 6, the "what" for a young boy on a hillside was his lunch: five barley loaves and two fish. Five thousand men (not to mention the women and children present, who typically were not counted in New Testament times) had listened most of the day to Jesus speak of hope and freedom and truth and light. They listened through lunchtime and on into the dinner hour without taking time to refuel. When Jesus' followers pointed this out to him, he told them to feed the people, which to the disciples seemed a ridiculous directive—until Jesus multiplied that young boy's lunch into a veritable smorgasbord for the hungry crowds. The boy's "what" fed tens of thousands of hungry men, women, and children.

So, what's my "what"?

The element of faith comes into play here. My "what" may not look like much to me. It may seem puny. It may look like no big deal, as if it couldn't make a dent. But when I put my "what" in Jesus' hands, it becomes enough.

I've experienced this over and over in parenting. I'll be running on empty—with a capital E—and then along comes a child needing my "what." So I offer it, and most of the time, it's enough. I remember staring into my pantry one night, hoping for dinner inspiration for my "starving" five-year-old son. Plunking down a plate of Top Ramen and chunk pineapple in front of him, I sat next to him, and we bowed our heads for grace. He looked up at me and said, "You are the best cook in the world, Mom—no, you're the best *mom* in the world!" *Go figure*, I thought.

I actually think back on this put-my-what-in-Jesus'-hands principle a lot as a mom, even though my children are adults now. I don't have enough. I can't make a dent, so to speak. I can't pay off their debts. I can't find them jobs. I can't heal their wounds from painful relationships. But I *can* invest in their lives, with faith and trust that God will match my offering to the need before me.

What if I did what is before *me* today? What if I let go of the pressure to do *everything* I could and instead did the *one* thing I could do now? That helps. It takes the focus off of giving *everything* and places it on giving *the one thing* that would matter right now, in this moment. After all, on another occasion, Jesus commended Mary for choosing to do the "*one* thing worth being concerned about" when she sat and learned at his feet (Luke 10:42, emphasis added). I could keep my grandson for the evening to give my daughter and her husband a "free" date night. I could pick up a birthday balloon for a coworker. I could offer a sincere compliment to the person in line behind me. I could grab an extra burger so I'm not empty-handed at the traffic light where the homeless hang out. Those "whats" are not so big. Not so impossible. Not so crazy-beyond-my-capacity. But will they be enough?

Sometimes I think that if I don't give *everything*, I'm somehow cheating God. I'm compromising. I'm selling out. I'm lazy and corrupt and just basic "slime." It's stunning to realize how easy it is to do *nothing* because I self-incriminate about not doing *everything*!

In most circles, some 80 percent of the people do only 20 percent of the work, and the remaining 20 percent do 80 percent of the work. In whichever slot we fall—"underly overinvolved" or "overly underinvolved"—we focus either on *nothing* or on *everything* and miss seeing our "what," the slot that lies between nothing and everything, where we live out our lives most of the time.

It also helps to remember that most of the time we don't know the importance of our "what" until after we do it. And sometimes not until *way* after we do it. A coworker stopped me in the hall to tell me that one day a few months ago, when I had simply stopped to ask about her and then had actually listened to her response, she'd been really close to quitting. I'm ever so glad now that I did that, even though I had no idea how much it was needed at the time.

What's my "what"? Maybe it depends on the moment and on what is needed in that moment. What if I give connection and empathy to someone who needs to feel heard and understood? At times that's really "expensive" for me. Most of the time, I have no space in my life to listen. But I listen anyway. And that makes a difference.

● ● ●

Becky struggled to identify her "what" between lots of would-be "whats."

First it was a Friday-afternoon request in the hallway at school while she was picking up her second grader: "Can you bring a batch of cookies next Monday for the teachers?" She agreed and headed her child to the van to make the next stop.

Then it was a phone call from someone asking her to help out in the nursery on Sunday. It seemed the flu was going around, and the department head sounded desperate. Okay.

As they were pulling in the driveway, her preteen remembered a homework project that required poster board, so Becky put the car in reverse, backed out of the driveway, and headed to the store.

Later, when her husband fell asleep on the couch during the game and Becky saw his tired face, she went ahead and mowed the lawn, even though it was "his" job.

Dinnertime came and went. Dishes were done, and the laundry waited. But when she answered the phone, she heard her panicked neighbor's voice pleading with her to come babysit while they raced to the emergency room with one of their children, who'd apparently had some kind of seizure.

Leaving the piles of laundry, Becky did what she could. She hurried next door.

Which "what" was Becky's "what"? How do you know?

When I asked about her "what," she said that it wasn't until the very end of that Sunday night, when she'd reviewed a litany of "whats," that she realized it was this last one that had truly been the bull's-eye on her "what" target: The call from her neighbor, arising from their relationship, communicated a need that Becky alone could meet.

What is your "what"? My "what" may be different from your "what." And yours may not be the same all the time.

* * *

One night, after Bible Study, Kendall desperately needed to breast-feed her baby. But her friend was hurting, and Kendall was the only one her friend would open up to. Could Kendall sit with her in her car and listen, and then pray with her? Yes, she could. She grabbed the baby and the diaper bag, headed for the car, and did *what* she could.

● ● ●

Alexandra normally spent five dollars a week on a specialty coffee. It was her Friday-morning splurge. But one day she wondered, *What if I wrote a check for more than I normally give to a cause and then cut back on something for "me" to underwrite the extra amount?* After some consideration, she decided to take the money she would have spent on coffee and give it to MOPS (Mothers of Preschoolers), International. That's $20 a month, approximately $240 a year. Alexandra did *what* she could. And it added up.

● ● ●

Lisa asked herself, *What if I went through my closet and culled things I haven't worn for at least a year? Then, instead of just dropping them off at the thrift store, what if I thought of people who wear my size and really need those items and gave the clothes to them?* That's *what* she did.

My presence. My coffee money. My clothes. My "what" can change from day to day, even from minute to minute. I can discover my "what" when I attend to what is happening around me and to what is in my possession that can make a difference at a particular moment. What if I did *what* I could?

*What if . . . I did what **I** could?*

What if I offered my story and my skills?

What if I didn't wait until I had it right or finished or perfect?

What if I believed God loved me so much that I wanted to love him back by doing what I could?

10
What If . . .
*I Did What **I** Could?*

I'm a woman, created by God, shaped by life, and equipped by all I've experienced. What if I invested *me*—who God has made me to be and how my relationship with Jesus is making me today—in what I am facing?

It was 1989. I remember that my hand was on the phone and I was preparing to make a call. I was more than a bit nervous. I had been hosting a radio program for a local grad school, and the decision had been made to drop it for budgetary reasons. But with about five years of programming already "in the can," I thought it would be silly to just let it go, and I very much wanted to see the program adopted by another institution. I also needed the money.

So with my hand on the phone, I prayed that God would make a way for the program to continue. It would take some major miracle work on God's part. I was a nobody. Who would want that program?

Just as I was ready to punch in the number, the phone rang. I jumped—answered it, and discovered that the caller was a board member of MOPS International (a lifestyle evangelism and leadership-development ministry for moms of preschool age children), inquiring about my interest in the position they had open for president—of the whole shebang. The person chosen would be the first president of the grassroots effort that had begun some fifteen years earlier.

Me? Ha! Me? The daughter of an alcoholic mother? Me? The mother of two young adopted children (three and five), who wasn't quite sure how well she was doing in that new role? Me? Lead an international mothering organization?

It sounded preposterous! But because of how the call had come, in the exact moment when I found myself at a juncture between one job and the next, I responded that I would pray about it and that I would be open to considering it.

I began to look—really look—at the mothers around me. In the grocery store one afternoon, with my own children leaning out of the cart to try to reach the temptations in the checkout line, I examined the other moms, in sweats, in jeans, in professional attire, juggling this and that and more, and all the while mothering their hearts out.

I felt God was saying to me, "Look at them. They have the same Swiss-cheese holes in their souls that you have in yours. Give to them out of all of you, out of what you know and what you don't know. Let even your deficits be your offering."

What if I did what *I* could? The question forced a response then. It still does today.

I, a daughter of divorce and alcoholism. The sister of multiple whole, half-, and stepsiblings. The wife of a man whose great love for me leaves me humbled. The mother of two children I didn't carry but could never lay down. A leader formed as much by codependent meanderings as by good, pure efforts.

What if I offered *my* unique offering, beginning right here and right now—honestly, unapologetically, and freely— because *I know that I know that I know* that I am loved, so much that I choose to live loved?

I served as president and CEO of MOPS International for twenty years. During my tenure, I invested my ability to speak persuasively in order to communicate the vision for the mission to others. I asked for and received loyalty from the staff and from the enormous wave of hundreds of thousands of moms, because I knew such a following was necessary for accomplishing the mission.

I made mistakes, lots of them. I plunged ahead when I should have waited. I was shortsighted because I thought I had the whole picture and I didn't. But in both my good moments and my not-so-good ones, in flush seasons and frugal ones, I gave *me* to the ministry and watched God make *me* enough.

King David started out as a shepherd. As a boy, he protected his sheep from danger. In the lonely days and nights in the meadows, he leaned into his own Shepherd and received protection and provision. He drove lions and bears away from the flock, rescued lambs from their mouths, and fought and killed the predators with a club (see 1 Samuel 17:34-36). Anointed as king when he was just a teenager, he drew from this early experience as a shepherd when it came to protecting his people: He picked up five stones, hurled one from his sling, and knocked a giant out cold. He did what he could.

Later in his life, resting on his earlier accomplishments, he foolishly gave in to his own passions with Bathsheba, committing first adultery and then murder. Yet from such a season of blunder, God later brought forth David's successor, Solomon, who became known as the wisest king of Israel, responsible for beginning the collection of our "proverbial" wisdom.

When we live loved, we splash in the puddle of our personhood, and smeared with the stains of our humanity, we rise to find God forming all of what we are into an offering that somehow shapes the world around us for good.

What would it mean for you to do what *you* could? You, the child of _____, or the sibling of _____, or the spouse of _____, or the parent of _____, or the grandparent of _____. What do you bring to this world in the offering of *you*? How has God redeemed who *you* are in such a way that it can be invested, all of it, for his purposes? How does he want to meet you in the messiness of who *you* are in order to shape your unique investment?

If you're not sure, put the book down for a minute, and really think about what *you* can offer. . . .

Are you back? I can hear your objections now: Oh no, you say. You don't know what I've done—the choices, the messes, the secrets. Why, just yesterday—*no way*. It's too messy. I don't want to get involved. I might get hurt, and I'm *done* with getting hurt.

Forget it, you decide. You'd rather go it alone— uninvolved, controlling the flow of life and love and therefore the ramifications for your soul.

I know. In the months that preceded our move into our current home, I had a dream. Or maybe I should say I encountered the first episode of what would become a recurring dream. Our children were teens, busy with school and friends and all that went with them. Our home was under construction, and more than once I had walked through the framed-out floor plan of our new home, imagining what would go where. Life was chaotic. It's no wonder even my sleep was filled with dreams about planning and preparing.

One night, a dream took me on a tour up the wooden stairs to the newly erected walls that formed the bedrooms. In my dream, God said to me, "These rooms are for your daughter and her baby."

"She isn't pregnant!" I answered.

"Yes, she is," came the reply.

When I awoke, I shook off the dream, dismissing it as a consequence of too much stress, and went about my day as usual.

Another night not long after, I dreamed again. This time I was walking with God in the basement of the unfinished house. Again I heard him say, "These rooms are for your daughter and her baby."

"No, she's not pregnant," I replied, but when I awoke, I wondered. . . .

Later that day, when my daughter approached me saying that she felt "funny," I drew a deep breath and asked her if she could be pregnant. To my stunned surprise, she nodded. Hours later I sat with her in the doctor's office as the results of a test registered—and so did the reality.

Like most moms who think their kids would never go in such a direction, I flipped out. It didn't help that I was heading up a mothering organization. I didn't want my daughter to be pregnant. I didn't want to be a grandmother. I didn't want my teenage son, a few years younger than my daughter, to suddenly become an uncle. No.

I didn't feel loved, nor did I want to live loved. I wanted to hide my daughter, my family, and me. I didn't want to lead a mothering organization, involving zillions of moms just setting out on the journey of motherhood, while making my way through what I defined as "ruin."

My daughter had her baby, and she and her son lived upstairs for the first two and a half years of his life—in the very rooms that it seemed God had set apart for them. My husband and I parented our daughter and grandparented our grandson, and when they eventually moved out on their own, we continued to do so over the two-mile distance that stretched between us. Later, she married, and they became a family—my grandson, my daughter, and her new husband.

Gradually—make sure you note that word *gradually*—I realized that I'd been given a relationship with yet one more mother of preschool-age children, that she'd been "born" right under my own roof, and that her presence in my days would provide a deeper understanding of the audience I served.

But this experience wasn't just about other people. It was also about me. Just as space had been created in our new home for my enlarged family, space was also being created in *me*. Over time, I began to understand how even in this unexpected "expectancy," there was so much *good*. So much *more*. So much *love* to live out.

I now had even more *me* to offer. What if I did what *I* could?

We sometimes forget that doing what *we* could means living loved. It's not always easy, or even comfortable. But when our action arises out of a relationship of love, stunning possibilities emerge. Fear fades into the background. Options grow. Choices flow. Suddenly we know—and so we go.

Layer after layer, love builds our lives, and our lives build our love. Today we have more to offer than we did last week or last year or a decade ago.

When I came into marriage, I had a rather meager version of love to share: romantic, in the moment, restricted by my own limits. Thirty years later I am fuller, freer, more forgiving. I forget to keep score—finally. I am now able to move beyond annoyance over my husband's quirks, understanding that they are just part of him and who he is rather than elements in some grand scheme of selfishness, out to take me over and win.

In my leadership, I move less definitively and work to allow greater room for the contributions of others. I pause to listen more. I ask questions and leave blank spaces.

My mothering is now more like "familying." Rather than try to maintain the tightly knit foursome of our early years, when I sweated every stitch of my efforts and tied us together with a furious commitment, today I am able to relax in the assurance that who we are has already been woven. We can stretch more than we could ever imagine. The comings— planned and unplanned—won't ruin the structure. The goings won't tear us apart beyond the healing power of love.

Try combing through the various layers of *you*. (It's not necessary to pull out your Myers-Briggs Type Indicator or do an online inventory of your skill set. Just take a look at *you* and what *you* can offer.) What if *you* did what only *you* could do? What would happen that could have happened no other way? What could occur through *you*? What might develop in *you* if *you* did what *you* could?

We so often count ourselves short. We tend to compartmentalize the public from the private, the loser from the winner, and thus, when we consider what there is in ourselves that we might bring out to meet a need, we tally up short. We discount or dismiss what we see as "negatives" in ourselves, when they actually form many of the things we have to offer. Who better to help one alcoholic than a recovering alcoholic? Who else can grasp the pain of grief like another who has wailed in anguish? Who else can pave the way toward hope for an incest survivor like another survivor who has found her way?

Parenting challenges, failed relationships, territory recovered from addictions, financial losses, even convicted time served—*all* of the experiences in the *all* of you and me make up what we bring to a moment.

Only I could be my daughter's and son's mother. Only I can be my grandson's "Yia Yia." Only I can be married to my husband, befriend my coworker who develops cancer in midlife, and invest who I have become where I am called to be.

What if I did what *I* could?

*What if . . . I did what I **could**?*
What if I acted with what I have?
What if I acted right where I am?
What if I acted because it might
    matter?

11
What If . . .
*I Did What I **Could**?*

What if I took stock of my offerings and humbly but realistically grabbed hold of what I *could* do—and did it, without holding back? Even if it made little sense to those around me but all the sense in the world to God? How could I wholeheartedly let God love me and then love him back, if I did what I *could*?

"Leave her alone." That's what Jesus said to the room filled with criticism. In other words, "Quit bothering her." I turn the eyes of my imagination away from Jesus and look back at Mary, seeing her the way he sees her: earnest and pure; her action in the moment, beautiful.

I am struck by his command: "Leave her alone."
Her who?
Well, Mary, of course, but also *you*.
Dear one, leave *you* alone. Leave yourself alone. Quit

bothering the *her* that is *you*. Stop needling her, judging her, messing with her, being embarrassed by her. Don't tie her up in knots and make her all anxious and sweaty. Silence the stream of self-editing that tells her that she's not enough, that she's silly or worthless, that she has really bad ideas and is way out of line. Take your hands off her! Let her be!

That's pretty much what Jesus was saying—*is* saying now: "Let her bring what she possesses to me. Let her do what she *could*. Let her give, whatever it is."

That really makes me think.

What if I acted with what I have? What if I did what I could by giving what I think I can't live without? Could I live without another pair of black shoes? Could I make out a check for the same amount as my mortgage this month and invest in a school in India? I wonder . . .

Way back in my early working days, a young mom who worked in our office mentioned her family's struggle to make ends meet. It was a casual comment, made after she arrived one day and hung her stained coat on a hook in her office. Actually, it was more of a parka. It didn't really "work" for a dress coat, and in those days people wore dress coats to work.

Later that week, I was at the mall and noticed in a store window a beautiful pink coat. A wool, dress-length coat. I didn't even stop to think. I went into the store, bought the coat, and asked that it be shipped to our office. When it arrived, I didn't give myself away, but I did share her joy and surprise as she put on the coat and twirled in front of the rest of the staff.

I'm not telling on myself now to make you think I'm

cool. I'm telling you this now because in trying to make it clear that there is a sacrificial element to doing what you can, I want you to understand that the level of sacrifice doesn't have to take the action beyond what is possible. It was possible for me to pay for the pink coat. Yes, I had less left to spend for the rest of the month after doing so. But the expenditure was possible, and from that possibility, I made the investment.

Sometimes acting with what we have means we spend money. Other times we invest less tangible assets, such as love, time, or energy.

Linda, a friend who was dying of cancer, called me and in her usual forthright manner asked if I would handle her funeral service. By *handle*, she meant "speak at it." I'd never before "done" a funeral. I had been to them, of course, but I'd never offered more than a handful of wadded tissues as my role.

My friend's death was imminent. My schedule was packed. My only remaining parent was also hovering near death. My emotions were torn. My heart was heavy. And then I considered all the "but, but, buts" on my list and moved beyond them to the *could* in the question. *Could* I do this thing for her?

Instead of focusing on what I didn't have, I took inventory of me—of what I did have. Speaking at the service would cost me, but it was something I "had." Yes, I could.

After a long and rather exhausting week of meetings, I drove down to visit with Linda at her daughter's house. I had fretted over how I would honor her desires and give an accurate representation of her life. I hadn't known her except through work, and work is only one facet of a person's life. What in the world could I say to comfort her family and friends? When would I have time to compose some kind of message that would offer the hope they needed and deserved?

When I arrived, I was escorted to the living room, where Linda lay on a hospital bed. I scooted a chair close and leaned in as she spoke. Clearly in pain, she instructed me to speak from Hebrews 11:1: "Faith is the confidence that what we hope for will actually happen; it gives us assurance about things we cannot see."

At least I had a verse to work from, but now what?

I decided to go the question route. In interview style, I asked about her faith. What mattered to her and what didn't? When had she felt closest to God and when the furthest from him? What did she think heaven would be like, and how did she hold on to her hope for it?

After just twenty minutes, I had the message. Linda had preached it straight to me. All I had to do was write it down and get ready to speak it for her.

As Jesus had told the roomful of objectors, I had to "leave her alone." When I quit "bothering" myself, I discovered that my friend had already given me what *she* had and then *I* had it to give to others after her death.

What if I acted where I was? What if I did what I could in front of others? What if I held up a placard on Martin Luther King Jr. Day, even though I'm white? What if I sat and listened to my Buddhist friend—just listened? What if I met the eyes of the guy holding a cardboard sign at the intersection and then rolled down my window and handed him a bill?

Leave her alone. Quit bothering her, and discover what it means to do what I *could*, what you *could*.

When my son was going through a particularly tough spell, I considered my possible responses: silence or cajoling or retaliation? Prayer, for sure. My husband and I talked it over, and over, and over. Finally we determined that our best response was to err on the side of love. Again and again and again we chose to make sure that if our son ever looked back and questioned his choices, he would always see us forgiving, accepting, and embracing, not necessarily every choice he made, but his being, his personhood, his value on this planet, and his relationship to us as son.

Not everyone agreed with our approach. Some feared that we were too forgiving, that we didn't show enough tough love. In middle-of-the-night moments, we, too, wondered, *Is this what we could do? Is this what we should do?*

Leave her alone. Quit bothering her—me. Stop picking at my shortcomings, and instead, let myself be enough. I do what I *could*. I act with what I have. I act where I am. I act because it just might matter.

What if you did what you *could*? What if you quit bothering yourself with criticism and negative judgments? Tell the Judas voice in your head to leave your Mary alone. Now. "Let the children come to me. Don't stop them! For the Kingdom of God belongs to those who are like these children" (Luke 18:16).

What do you have? Maybe it's an open hand. Maybe it's ten extra minutes or fifty bucks. Or pet supplies left over after your dog died a while back. Whatever it is, act with it.

What neat thing might happen if you act on something that really matters? Go for it.

Imagine: *What might happen if I did what I could? How would I be changed? How would others be changed? How would Jesus be loved? How might others see the gospel—see Jesus—if I did what I could?*

What if I did what I could?
*   As a result of my action, someone*
*   would be helped.*
*   As a result of my action, I would be*
*   better.*
*   As a result of my action, the world*
*   would be better.*

What if I had a relationship that resulted
*   in a response?*

12
What If I Did What I Could?

What if I lived each day with the commitment to do what I could in that day, to know that I am loved by Jesus and to love him back?

I might schedule a meeting with the principal and press the school to provide the special services I know my child requires in order to be the best he can be.

I might go on bed rest during a difficult pregnancy in order to give the life inside of me a chance at life outside of me.

I might apologize to a friend I wounded.

I might resign from my job and make more time for my kids.

I might go back to work in order to provide more resources for my kids.

I might stay married.

I might forgive my mother.

I might forgive myself.

I might share my story—my struggle—my sins—in public so that others might hear that the God who has helped me can help them.

I might tithe more than makes sense but not more than I really can afford.

I might adopt a child.

I might bite my tongue instead of speaking.

I might vote.

I might make a cup of cocoa for my husband and take it to him while he watches TV. Not because he asked for it or because I need to be in his good graces. Just because.

I might get off the couch and go for a walk with my daughter.

What if I did what I could?

One Monday morning, a woman I didn't know well e-mailed me a prayer update about her young teen daughter who had become a mother. The woman ended her e-mail with a line that pretty much said she didn't have anyone to talk to. I stared at the words. I knew she worked near my office. I looked at the clock and scrolled through my calendar, where I found a free hour—just thirty minutes from then. I e-mailed her and asked her to meet for coffee. I had no idea what I'd say to her, but I drove to the coffee shop. I didn't become her sole support. I didn't promise to see her every week. I didn't fix her life. But I sat and listened. I did what I could.

Once, when my grandson was sleeping over at our house, I awoke in the middle of the night and climbed the stairs to check on him. The baby monitor had been quiet, but, of course, you never know for sure unless you check. As I stood looking at him, I noticed that his body seemed rigid, so I reached out my hand to pat his back—a big mistake for a woman who hoped to return to sleep that night. His little head shot up, and he looked at me. "Are you okay?" I asked.

"No, Yia Yia. My tummy hurts." After checking to see if he needed to throw up or something, I straightened back up. Then came the question: "Yia Yia, could you lie down with me?"

I thought about his question. *Could* I lie down with him? The question wasn't, "Will you stay up all night and never get any sleep yourself and never go back to your own bed?" No, the question was, "Could you lie down with me?"

Yes, I could. I climbed over the twin bed's safety bar and lay down with my grandson. I did what I could.

On another occasion, I stopped at Marshalls, looking for something to wear at my next speaking engagement. I found a skirt—shortish, blue and black and gray—that was just right to go with the top I'd already scored on sale. The skirt's price tag read $69.99. That was too much, and definitely more than I like to pay.

But I headed to the checkout anyway, where I plunked down the skirt along with several other clearance doodads I had found in the gift department.

"That'll be $32.95," the clerk announced.

"Did you get the skirt?" I asked.

"Yes," he answered.

"Did you take the security sensor off?"

He patted his hand over the garment. "Yes," he said.

"Okay." I swiped my credit card while a lump started in my throat. *Wow! That skirt was nearly seventy dollars, and I think I'm getting it for, like, nothing!* Then that thought slammed right up against the next one: *That's stealing, darling. That total can't be right. Say something.*

I'll wait and check the receipt—maybe it was more discounted than I thought.

Say something.

No.

Back and forth it went, the arguing in my head. I made it all the way out of the store and into my car, where I checked the receipt. The skirt wasn't listed. I was really hoping that the next thought—*It's too late to change now*—would kick in, but it didn't. I was hoping the arguing would stop once I got the skirt home and hung safely inside my closet. It didn't.

And then I remembered that I was planning to wear the skirt to a speaking engagement and that God would be completely justified in striking me dead on the spot if I stood and proclaimed his Word in a stolen skirt! I would just have to go back to the store the next day and fess up—which I did.

It is *so* miserable to hand your credit card and receipt over to a clerk who couldn't care less, endure her incredulous stare, and know that $69.99 is being added to your card balance.

The clerk wasn't at all impressed that I had returned to make things right. If I had been in her position, I would have called the manager and reported over the loudspeaker the high level of integrity my customer had. I might even have given her a gift card good for twenty-five dollars toward a future purchase.

I honestly confess that I *so* didn't want to do what I could in that situation. But I did it.

What if every day I did what I could? What if every day I did what I could because I'm so convinced that Jesus loves me? What if the way I love Jesus in return for his loving me is to do what I could? What if the way Jesus shows the gospel to this world is sometimes through *me*—doing what I could?

As we clearly see in the story of Mary of Bethany, a relationship with Jesus results in a response. But just as Mary had no control over how her action would be received by those who observed it, I'm not able to control others' reactions to my response.

I might be rejected. Others might decide that my doing what I could is excessive, wasteful, inappropriate, or an all-about-me attempt to get attention.

I might be ridiculed: Ha! Who do you think you are with all this "she did what she could" stuff?

I might be honored.

I might make Jesus smile. I might demonstrate my extreme gratitude for his loving me by loving him back in a moment when my action means something to his people and his planet and, therefore, to him.

I'm not responsible for the response to my response. I'm just invited to respond. When I do what I could, I tell the Good News of the gospel to the world around me. A relationship that results in a response is a beautiful thing. I am changed, and I change my world. *When I do what I could.*

PART 3

What If We Did What We Could?

What if . . . **we** did what **we** could?
What could we all accomplish if all of
us did what we could?
What could we do together that we
couldn't do alone?
What if I did what I could and you did
what you could and then we did
what we could?

13
What If . . .
We Did What We Could?

We who? You plus me equals we.

What if *we* did what *we* could? What could we do together that we couldn't do alone?

The answer to that question isn't so hard: We could do lots. I can do only what I can do: reach out to the folks on my street, at my job, in my marketplace, in my kids' school, and in my church with my skills and my story and my money and my perspective. If I did what I could, I could do quite a bit. But I couldn't do nearly as much as if together *we* did what *we* could.

Think about it! Imagine what could happen if we added just what I could do to what you could do. And then you and I added a few more of us: people in the book club, the office, the church, the neighborhood, my city, your city, the state.

Five plus 15 plus 50 plus 100 plus 1,000 plus 5,000 plus 10,000 plus 50,000 plus 100,000 plus 1,000,000.

What if *we* did what *we* could?

What could we *all* accomplish if each one of us did what she could and then *we* added all these efforts together? This is the body of Christ in action—uniquely called to both an individual and a corporate investment of who *we* are.

My friend Debbie loves stirring up interest in global issues, believing that God's passion is for the world—all of it. She wants to get Christians involved with world issues. Her concern is both personal and planetwide. So she talks to anyone who will listen and offers to strategize with those people to connect others in conversations. Her dream is to set up ongoing groups in churches for prayer, discussion, and eventually involvement. What if there were a Debbie in every church?

Tracy believes that God gave the earth to people to enjoy and to steward. Only a few months after she was hired, she asked the president of her company for permission to spearhead a recycling program. Today the company has shredders for paper and recycling bins for plastic, cardboard, glass, and other items stationed all around the office building. What if there were a Tracy in every office?

Another friend, Debbie, and her husband, Rick, heard about women in undeveloped countries who have no supplies for attending to the most basic daily responsibilities, like washing clothes and preparing food. Then they discovered Global Action, a ministry organization that sends Buckets of Love to impoverished women. The actual buckets are filled with basic supplies such as soap, washcloths, toothbrushes and toothpaste, tape, twine, simple toys for children, and other necessary items, fourteen in all. Rick and Debbie funded several buckets. And then they replaced company-client Christmas gifts with notifications that they were funding more. What if there were a Rick and Debbie in every business?

Doug and Cindy have a passion for healthy marriages. As expatriates, they spent nearly a decade in the United Kingdom, where they gathered friends at a local pub every week to dive into discussions about how marriage really works. Now back in the States, they're recreating this effort in a local bar. Couples are coming—and growing in their relationships. What if there were a Doug and Cindy in every bar?

One. 15. 60. 150. 3,200. 10,683. What could we *all* accomplish if one or two or three of us did what we could and then *we* added our efforts together?

> *Amor mundi* [love for the world] [is] our being quickened to a divine but painful compassion for the world. . . . And it is *amor mundi* that compels millions of ordinary folk like you and me to minister life in Christ' s good name to our neighbor, our *nigh-bor*: "the person who is near us."[1]
> —Richard Foster

SDWSC. We decide the concept is exciting and highly motivational. We can hardly wait to get started. And so, full of good intentions, we dive in and are SDWSC-ing away when *bam!*—we're blindsided by criticism. We get grief instead of support.

Have you ever run into people who demand that you

believe everything the way they believe it or you can't be part of their "we"? Have you ever experienced what it feels like to be excluded from the great Christian "we"?

Mary nearly was. A roomful of followers collectively gasped at her action and then troubled her to the point of rejection. If the folks at that dinner party had had their way, Mary would never have acted at all, her gift of anointing Jesus' body before his death scuttled before it could even get away from the dock. But Jesus interceded. He pronounced her action beautiful and paired it with the preaching of the Good News for all time.

How often we use our *we* to cripple the body of Christ rather than to release God's power in us and through us: Believe the way *we* believe. Attack the "enemies" *we* attack. Parent the way *we* parent. Support the causes *we* support. Be like us. Be *we*, not them. They do things *we* don't do. They believe things *we* don't believe. They go places *we* don't go. They hang out with other "thems." They can't be *we*.

But just as Jesus interceded for Mary, he intercedes for us. A relationship with Jesus results in a response. When *we* are loved, *we* can live loved.

Most people in my generation have grown up believing that a Christian is defined by what he or she doesn't do. We are beginning to understand that a Christian is better defined as someone who does certain behaviors that are reflective of love, mercy, justice, and compassion.
—Jena Nardella, executive director, Blood:Water Mission, Nashville, Tennessee

Occasionally in the ministry world, ultimatums are delivered, muscles are flexed, and threats are made: Match our political agenda, or you're out. Parrot our passions, or you won't sell books in our circles. Say the words the way we say them, or you won't have a speaking platform with us.

What ministry leader hasn't experienced the pain of diminished Kingdom impact because some powerful part of the Kingdom decided that leader wasn't "we"? It's very common.

I once bumped up against a ministry giant in just such a scenario. When our board members received an ultimatum, they refused to bend to it. Our board believed that the other ministry's mission—while Kingdom-centered and valid—wasn't our mission. Strong convictions held that taking on their mission as ours would actually hamper our efforts to accomplish what God had called us to do. When the ministry giant withdrew its support, we lost out big-time. It hurt—corporately and personally. The wound was painful, heart-heavy, and hard to bear.

Notice all the *we*'s and *they*'s in this language. Isn't this where such thinking leads us? To focus on opposing one another rather than on fulfilling our common Kingdom purposes?

During that difficult season, an image came to me that helped me to see the Kingdom of God as a whole posse of individuals who together form a varied and multifaceted community. I saw thousands of individual believers, standing side by side in a circle and facing *out* rather than each other. As people looked out to the Kingdom cause directly in front of them—their slice of the whole Kingdom effort—they could see only those people who stood next to them.

As they looked to the right and to the left, they were strengthened by the sight of the ones they saw fighting beside them. But from where they stood, they concluded that those fighting side by side with them were the *only* ones fighting for the Kingdom. Aside from their comrades beside them, they believed they were alone in the battle. Anyone who wasn't standing right beside them was not fighting the cause to which they were committed and, in fact, was not fighting for the Kingdom at all.

As I thought about that image, I was struck by the fact that if we were just to turn and look over our shoulders— all of us—we would see that none of us is alone. Thousands and millions of brothers and sisters are standing along the Kingdom circle, addressing *their* particular issues and causes in their slice of the Kingdom, their part of the overall *we*.

In order to understand both the uniqueness and the magnitude of Kingdom calls, we have to look beyond those at our sides. We have to look over our shoulders and take in all those who "have our backs." Only then can we begin to understand the great communal effort that is taking place as one after another *we* respond to our own relationships with Jesus.

While the power of one is impressive, the power of community is awe-inspiring.
—Gloria Luna, director, Office of Social Advocacy, Catholic Charities, Archdiocese of Miami, Florida

Let me be clear. The essentials regarding the tenets of our faith in Christ—our beliefs about what makes Christianity Christianity and Christians Christians—are the foundation of *we*. But the specifics related to how each of us actively responds to our relationship with Jesus can vary from individual to individual and from call to call. Christ calls us into a relationship with him. He is the source of our offerings, of our actions. Each relationship results in a response that will be personal and contextualized in the world in which *we* live.

SDWSC is a powerful response to a relationship of healing that Jesus paired with the gospel for all time. She did what she could.

> The greatest social need in the world today is not HIV/AIDS outreach. It's not hunger. It's not global warming. Not ending poverty or eliminating malaria or tuberculosis. Not clean water. Not racial reconciliation. Not sexual trafficking. Not abortion. And it's not peace in the Middle East, and not even world peace. . . . None of [our] good works—nay, great works—deal with the most profound social problem facing humankind. That social problem is alienation from God.[2]

A relationship with Jesus is radical and transformational. We are changed by this relationship. And when we are changed, we want to change our world. Our relationship results in a response.

> There are two conversions in life: coming to Christ and then reformation—doing something about it.[3]
> —Rick Warren

All of us who sit at the feet of Jesus and are changed by his love are destined—no, *called*—to move on to the second conversion of expressing our faith in our actions. To do what we could.

> Caring for the suffering is not optional, and it's not for just a certain group of people. It should be a hallmark of our faith.[4]
> —Kay Warren

It's vital that each one of us do what *we* individually could. It is also vital that *we* do what *we* could together and that we respect how others do what they could so that *we* are all doing what *we* could. We don't have to be the same to be *we*. We don't have to agree with each other's finer points of theology to serve a meal to the hungry. We don't have to tackle the same issues at the same moment with the same verbiage in order for God's Kingdom to advance. In fact, in many cases we will have less impact if we all do the same thing than we would if we each did what we could alone and then all our efforts were added to a communal *we*.

What could we all accomplish if each one of us did what we could? I might minister to moms. You might stand against abuse. He feeds the hungry. She works for justice. They advocate for the homeless. Together, we might change the world. Many acts. One we.

> The human body has many parts, but the many parts make up one whole body. . . . If the whole body were an eye, how would you hear? Or if your whole body were an ear, how

would you smell anything? But our bodies have many parts, and God has put each part just where he wants it. How strange a body would be if it had only one part! Yes, there are many parts, but only one body.
—I Corinthians 12:12, 17-20

She did what she could. One girl entered a relationship with Jesus, and because a relationship with Jesus results in a response, she did what she could. She lived loved. Jesus invites us to do the same. He beckons us to a relationship with him, a relationship that results in a response, an action. Going. Doing. Giving. Loving. When we know Jesus and are known by him, we can live loved—all of us. Individually and together. You. And me. *We.*

What if . . . *we* did what *we* could?

What if we did what we could?
   How would we change?
   How would we change our world?

14
What If We Did
What We Could?

What if I did what I could and you did what you could and then we did what we could—all of us?

There are days when it all seems so impossible, like the evening I watched *NBC Nightly News* with Brian Williams and learned of the plight of special needs adults in Serbia.

Most of us care, remember? We really do. We care about our own lives, for sure, and also about the lives of those around us. We care about poverty and injustice, about orphans and the sick. We care about the folks who live and work alongside us and about what happens in their families and their hearts and their heads.

We care. But too often we stop there because we think that in order for it to count, to make a difference that matters, we have to do something *big*. Or *everything we could do*. Or something no one else has done.

But as we've seen, that's not true. Five letters representing five words make a world of difference. *SDWSC*. She did what she could.

From the online World Vision HIV/AIDS exhibit, I learned that thirty-three million people are living with HIV.[1] Six thousand people die every day. Whole generations have been lost. As I listened to Gary Haugen of the International Justice Mission, I discovered that twenty-seven million people are living in slavery and two million children exist in forced prostitution. Twenty-four thousand children die of starvation *every day*.

How can this be?

It's too much. Most of us do well just to get through to dinner, bath time, and bedtime. We hold the future in our hands as we rock our babies, love our little ones, nurture them with everything we have, and pray they will grow to be healthy, contributing, God-loving adults.

That's a lot—isn't it?

Yes, it's a lot. But what if each of us, you and I, did what we could? How might our actions be paired with the gospel so that people could see Jesus?

What if . . .

● ● ●

Karen lost one of her six children. Perhaps a better way to put it is that if all of Karen's children had lived, she would have six rather than five. Or would she even have the five without the loss of the one?

First came a son. Then another son, who lived only a few hours. Then a healthy boy. Then a gorgeous baby girl. Throughout the journey into—and out of—parenthood, a desire to adopt had grown in Karen's and her husband's hearts.

As the years passed, Karen continued to yearn for children she didn't know, had never seen. At first she and her husband were drawn to Brazil and journeyed there to investigate the possibility of adoption. But they found the doors closed, and they obligingly turned toward home, only to find their hearts leapfrogging across the Atlantic toward Africa. They researched, prayed, waited, worked, mobilized to act in response to the HIV/AIDS pandemic. Fighting and finally winning, they adopted a brother and sister from Ethiopia.

Karen and her husband weren't completely selfless souls who, Mother Teresa–like, wanted to care for the orphans of the world. They were a couple in need of children to complete their family.

Three children instead of four led to five children instead of three. They did what they could.

● ● ●

Evan and his wife were returning from a weekend getaway. It had been fun—a treat, in fact. They had preboarded the plane and settled into their traveling postures: Evan at work on his laptop and his wife reading a magazine.

He looked up when her elbow dug into his side.

"Keep an eye on him!" she whispered, as an old, unshaven man wearing a plaid flannel shirt and sweatpants slid into the seat across the aisle from them and next to a young teenage girl. With the smell of alcohol heavy about him, he clutched a plastic shopping bag with a recognizable logo. Somehow Evan doubted that the man shopped there.

Everything seemed okay until midflight and a few drinks later, when the old man reached down unsteadily for his shopping bag and Evan caught sight of its contents: a plastic urinal.

Uh-oh.

"Sir." Evan leaned across the aisle. "You really can't use that here."

"Well, I can't make it to the lavatory. I'll fall on my a--." The man belched.

Evan closed his laptop, handed it to his wife, raised his tray table, unfastened his seat belt, and stood up. He leaned down and helped the man unbuckle his own seat belt and ushered him, weaving up the aisle, to the lavatory, where he helped him inside and then kept an eye out through the crack in the door until the old man was ready to return to his seat.

He did what he could.

● ● ●

Angel had been a leader in her MOPS group for more than a decade. She had a heart for the underdog: teen moms, moms on welfare, moms who lacked transportation, single moms, working moms, moms who were new in the community. Angel wanted all of them—every one of them—to discover the hope and help they could find in a relationship with Jesus.

She'd discovered him, herself, while in some pretty needy messes.

Years into various renditions of MOPS, Angel looked around and asked herself, *Where else on earth are there mothers?* To Angel's surprise, God directed her to consider moms who were incarcerated.

She contacted the sheriff at the Orange County correctional facility, near where she lived. She discovered that within the inmate population there was a large concentration of moms of young children. She asked for, and was granted, the opportunity to start a MOPS group for these women. And week after week, Angel and her team of helpers check their purses and belongings on one side of a reinforced door and then walk through it to bring hope and healing to the moms on the other side.

She did what she could.

● ● ●

Joanna needed volunteer hours for her high school service record. As an underclassman she chose ESL—English as a Second Language—and began tutoring women from Burma/Myanmar and Nigeria.

One woman told her, "I thought all Americans had guns. I was wrong. You've shown me love." What began as a high-school graduation requirement grabbed at Joanna's heart and became a passion.

As she prepared to finish her senior year, it became important to her that this program continue—and that the impact on her peers who would participate would be as great as it had been on her. So Joanna spent the remaining months of high school finding a replacement for herself and was able to link a local graduate equivalency diploma (GED) program to the ESL classes as well. She hadn't thought her volunteering would matter so very much—until it did.

So she did what she could.

● ● ●

After what seemed a "routine" hysterectomy, Jane discovered she had cancer, an aggressive, deadly cancer of the blood. Vibrant Jane, in her early sixties, was still teaching kindergarten at the private school she'd helped found more than twenty years earlier. Her daughter was about to be married, her oldest son was about to make her a grandmother, and suddenly—Jane was dying.

Dying? No way!

After exhaustive and exhausting tests, Jane and her family came to terms with the poor prognosis, and Jane began treatment to prolong her life. Their goal was for Jane to attend her daughter's wedding and hold her grandbaby.

Because Jane needed emergency treatment to stem internal bleeding, she missed the wedding celebration. But her daughter and the entire wedding party brought the real wedding to Jane, the bride and groom exchanging vows in the hospital chapel before returning to the site of the wedding and the reception.

Then, on schedule, Jane welcomed her first grandson, joyed beyond belief at his arrival.

In an unexpected season when good things happened only rarely, Jane received a treatment that extended her life. Over a year past her diagnosis, Jane made her bed each morning and fixed dinner each night. She drove to the school she'd founded and volunteered two days a week because, she said, "The hardest part about cancer is having your purpose taken away."

Jane still had cancer. The prognosis was that she would have an indefinite but likely short period of time for productive contribution. So Jane invested.

She did what she could.

* * *

Lee worried about her son: single, young, still in school, and bumping along in and out of sobriety. She longed to see him whole—no, healed. Her own journey to recovery had taught her that providing that healing for her son was beyond her own ability. No, his healing would require a journey of his own.

Just then, he stumbled and fell again. As Lee stepped back out of his path, grieving his self-destruction, she wondered just how her efforts could ever make a difference. Three months later, as her son was leaving the court appointment where he'd faced some legal consequences for his drinking, he called her. He was admitting himself to an inpatient treatment facility. Would she keep his dog—his intimidating, ninety-pound, eighteen-month-old dog—during the same weeks her kitchen and family-room floors were undergoing reconstruction and she was also caring for her four-year-old grandson?

She would. She did what she could.

* * *

Every Friday at noon, Dennis, Sharon, and Bill met for a quick bite to eat and then set to work. Dennis took the left side of the sanctuary, Sharon took the middle, and Bill took the right. Methodically, sometimes painfully, they moved from row to row to row, checking the pencils and the prayer cards.

They replaced the pencils that had broken points with sharpened ones. If the prayer cards had been doodled on, they were thrown away, and new ones were put in their place.

To some, this weekly ritual might seem insignificant, even silly. But to this faithful trio, it meant volumes. They knew that each Sunday morning, someone—many someones—would reach for a pencil and a prayer card and jot down a need. They knew this because after the Sunday services, the same trio gathered the cards and handed them to the deacons for action.

They did what they could.

• • •

Valerie took her husband's place on a trip to Kenya scheduled for various high-ranking ministry leaders in their association. She had no idea what she'd discover, but sensing it would be a life-altering journey, she armed herself with a journal and an open spirit and prepared to record every element of the trip. Or so she thought. Much of the time her heart simply broke open and leaked in a trail of emotion.

When she returned, she was changed. She simply could not *not* act. Each day she awoke to images of cows. If she could send money for cows to the woman who had become wedged in Valerie's soul, that woman could not only survive but also begin to make her way toward a life of her own. But Valerie didn't have money. She was a simple American woman trying to make her way as well.

Little by little, the realization dawned on Valerie that she could do a lot—a little at a time. At the grocery store, she asked that the savings from using her frequent-customer card be given to her in cash rather than deducted from her bill. Then she stashed away that amount each week. She made a commitment to avoid buying new clothing for a period of time and pocketed that savings as well. She clipped coupons and shopped at flea markets for gifts. Eventually, when she finally counted out her savings, she found she had enough to buy a starter herd of cattle for her new African friend.

She did what she could.

• • •

He had captured her heart with just a smile, a dimpled, joy-filled, sunburst of a grin. Sharon had never before loved with such abandon—she abandoned her to-do list, her carefully scheduled workday, even her favorite TV programs. She left it all, over and over, for this little three-year-old wonder.

When her daughter had revealed her pregnancy, Sharon had been hesitant. Was this young woman ready to mother? Was Sharon herself old enough to be "grandmotherly"? Goodness!

Over the years, Sharon's resolve to keep her grandson at a bit of a distance had evaporated. She fairly *ate him up*, so delight-ful was the lavish yumminess he brought to her life. And yet she wondered: Would her daughter teach him the simple prayers so precious to childhood? Would she teach him about God, about his own need for faith?

And then the idea came to her. She could teach him *herself* if it was okay with her daughter—and it was! So she picked up a couple of books about Jesus, and on her grandson's next visit, she tentatively opened them with him. He loved them! She bowed her head and held his hands in hers over his dinner of chicken nuggets and fries and prayed out loud, inviting him to repeat after her. He did! She buckled him into a car seat and took him with her to church. He loved it! She taught him—bit by bit—about *her* love for Jesus and Jesus' love for *him*.

She did what she could.

• • •

Judy had prayed for her prodigal son, Josh, for two years before she shared her pain with a friend. Then, in just minutes, she discovered how very *not* alone she was in her struggle. Serving in an international ministry with her husband, she heard story after story of parents' hearts broken over their prodigal children.

So Judy launched a Web-based prayer effort that drew together parents from every part of the world to pray their wayward ones home.

She did what she could.

• • •

Rob had been in the consulting business for a long time, maybe even forty years. He helped with executive- and senior-level searches. He knew people *everywhere*. Now, just months after retiring from his full-time role, he found himself seated next to a woman in a transition from CEO to goodness-knows-what. He'd heard some version of her story many times, along with the tentative, exploratory questions she mulled over regarding what might be next.

He knew he could help. Although he didn't have specific

answers about what her next steps should be, he was well acquainted with the questions she asked—and with the process ahead of her as she sought the answers she needed.

Reaching for his wallet, he found one remaining—rather dog-eared—business card. As he held it out to his seatmate, he invited her to call him for a free consultation.

He did what he could.

• • •

Beth hoisted the box of Easter decorations onto her kitchen counter. Over the years she had collected five or six different styles of plastic eggs, with a dozen in each set. They were great for the egg hunts and allowed adults and children of all ages to run about crazily in search of a color-coded treasure.

As she laid out the eggs and matched them to her kids and grandkids, she realized she had an extra set. What to do?

Then Ericka, her nail tech, popped into her mind. Beth didn't know her well, but the last time she had her nails done, Ericka had shared her disappointment over the fact that the deal had fallen through on the house she'd hoped to buy for herself and her two-year-old son. And the fact that the guy she'd been seeing had turned out to be—well, she wasn't seeing him anymore.

Beth wondered what Ericka and her little boy were doing on Easter Sunday. She had Ericka's cell-phone number. She could dial it and invite them to come for the afternoon.

She did what she could.

• • •

She Did What She Could. Five words that have changed my life.

Have they changed yours?

It's time to put down the book and pick up the challenge. You don't have to start another nonprofit (though, of course, you could). You don't even have to get off the couch. Just pick up the phone.

You. Act out of who *you* are.

Do. Don't just think about it. *Do* it.

What. What's your *what*? What keeps you from doing your *what*?

You. The moment is uniquely before *you*. Act out of who you are now and the you God is making you to be.

Could. The opportunity is here, now. It matters. Do what you can do.

A relationship with Jesus results in a response. So go ahead. Get out there and live loved.

SDWSC.

Afterword

The SDWSC stories in this book are real stories. In some, the names and certain details have been changed to preserve anonymity. Other stories remain unchanged and have been included with permission.

The purpose of these stories is to demonstrate just how simple and yet profound an SDWSC moment can be.

As these five letters, representing five words, take root in your heart, you may discover one—or many—SDWSC stories of your own. When you do, please consider sharing them at www.shedidwhatshecould.com.

A relationship with Jesus results in a response.

Notes

Chapter 3: She Did *What* She Could

1. J. D. Douglas (revising ed.) and Merrill C. Tenney (general ed.), *The New International Dictionary of the Bible, Pictorial Edition* (Grand Rapids: Zondervan, 1987), 804.

Chapter 4: She Did What *She* Could

1. William Barclay, *The Gospel of Mark* (Philadelphia: Westminster Press, 1975), 326.

Chapter 13: What If . . . *We* Did What *We* Could?

1. Richard Foster, "Spiritual Formation Agenda," *Christianity Today* (January 2009): 33.
2. "The Greatest Social Need," editorial in *Christianity Today* (January 2009): 18.
3. Rick Warren, as quoted by Bill Hybels.
4. Kay Warren, "My Heart Has Been Broken by the Suffering of AIDS," interview by Connie Willems, *Discipleship Journal* (March/April 2008): 54.

Chapter 14: What If We Did What We Could?

1. See http://www.worldvisionexperience.org/learn_crisis.asp, accessed May 20, 2009.

she did what she could

STUDY GUIDE

HOW TO USE THE BOOK
AND STUDY GUIDE

The study guide is intended to augment the book. Intentionally, it does not exactly follow the order of the book but rather references content in order to take it to application.

Participants can read the book and then do the study guide with the videos* on the She Did What She Could website (www.sdwsc.com). Or, participants can read the book along with the study guide.

Page numbers that specifically reference the book can be found in the notes section of the study guide.

In addition, a broad reference from guide to book is as follows:

LESSON ONE
She Did What She Could: A Relationship with Jesus Results in a Response
Chapter 6 and also chapters 1–5

LESSON TWO
Who Did What She Could and Why: Live Loved
Chapter 4 and also chapters 1–6

LESSON THREE
What If I did What I Could?: How to Live Loved
Chapter 7 and also Chapters 7–12

LESSON FOUR
What If I Didn't Do What I Could?: Live with No Regrets
Chapter 8 and also chapters 7–12

LESSON FIVE
What If We Did What We Could?: You Plus Me Equals We
Chapter 13

LESSON SIX
What If We All Did What We Could?: The Power of "We"
Chapter 14

*Please note that Flash Media is necessary to view the videos. Videos are not available on personal mobile devices.

We hope this information frees you and your participants to enjoy the study. Please be sure to post your SDWSC stories to share the news of how God is working!

The SDWSC Team
www.sdwsc.com

She Did What She Could

A relationship with Jesus results in a response.

*"I don't have an amazing story of a ministry
I started, but the other day I was in the ninety-nine-
cent store and an old man came up to me and asked
if he could borrow a dollar to buy some food. I happened to have only one dollar in my wallet and gave
it to him. And that phrase came to mind: 'She did
what she could.' It wasn't much, but it was what
I had at the time."* —JAIMIE

Begin by watching the "Message from Elisa" video clip from the SDWSC website (www.sdwsc.com).

CONSIDER THIS

Do you see it? Do you see what she did in Mark 14:3-9?

> While he was in Bethany, reclining at the table in the home of Simon the Leper, a woman came with an alabaster jar of very expensive perfume, made of pure nard. She broke the jar and poured the perfume on his head.
>
> Some of those present were saying indignantly to one another, "Why this waste of perfume? It could have been sold for more than a year's wages and the money given to the poor." And they rebuked her harshly.
>
> "Leave her alone," said Jesus. "Why are you bothering her? She has done a beautiful thing to me. The poor you will always have with you, and you can help them any time you want. But you will not always have me. She did what she could. She poured perfume on my body beforehand to prepare for my burial. Truly I tell you, wherever the gospel is preached throughout the world, what she has done will also be told, in memory of her" (NIV).

Let's stop and ponder the first five words of verse 8.

She: God chose a girl. God chose a woman who acted on her love for him in response to his love for her. If this grabs your attention today, just imagine how God's choice sat with the crowd just after the crossroads of time between BC and AD, when women were little more than property. Slaves. Chattel. In fact, tradition held that each morning, Jewish males offered a blessing that thanked God for not making them Gentiles, slaves, or women (page 6).

In choosing a girl, Jesus made a radical choice to make a point with incredible significance. No matter what we think of ourselves, God has chosen us to do things with amazing significance. Your giftedness, experience, and financial status have little bearing. Neither does your age or appearance. Jesus didn't choose a girl—Mary—by accident. He chose a girl on purpose. He paired her action with the gospel that would be preached through all generations. Jesus witnessed many wonderful and worshipful deeds by both men and women. He chose to make a big deal out of this one.

Did: She acted. She didn't just think about acting. She didn't act out of obligation. She didn't let others act for her. She didn't wait to be invited (page 9).

Doing something is important. Simply moving into action is vital. But so is attitude. Mary offered her perfume genuinely, without regrets. Her action was not part of a reward system or a tally of deeds. Her action was intentional, not rash and last minute. She didn't know the outcome, but that wasn't important. It's easy to have good ideas but much harder to act on them. Mary walked into a room of people, many who would not understand her intentions or her reasoning. She knew she was taking a risk. She also knew she was loved. Her action was in response to the love she'd been shown by Jesus.

What: She did *what* she could. Not *all* she could. Rather than give this—and that—and then some more, only to eventually fall, spent, at his feet, she gave what she could and left it at that. Enough. A lot. Just right. She chose *what* she could—and gave it ungrudgingly (page 17).

Mary didn't empty her closet and cupboards. She didn't paint or write or draw. She didn't accompany her gift with beautiful singing or an inspiring dance. She could have, perhaps. She just simply and authentically did what she could. Her response came from her relationship with Jesus. This time she gave a lot. But that's not what Jesus honored. He simply said, "She did a beautiful thing. She did what she could." He noticed that it was just what was needed at that particular moment.

She: She was a specific woman with a specific story who acted out of the particulars of her life. She acted because she knew she was loved and wanted to love back (page 19).

Her story, her experiences, her possessions, her giftedness, her circle of friends. These were the particulars of her life. She looked around at what she had and gave from that. She didn't try to be someone she wasn't. She could have prepared an incredible meal, but that was Martha's gifting. She could have stood at the door and welcomed everyone and washed their feet, but that wasn't her calling. She was Mary and she had a special jar of nard. She had a love for Jesus because of the love he had given to her and her family. Not only had Jesus encouraged Mary, he had healed her father, discipled her sister, and raised her brother. So she did what she could in a way that demonstrated her love.

Could: She acted with what she had. Mary grabbed hold of what she possessed—what was within her reach, under her power, obedient to her control—and she invested it. She did what she could with what she had to work with. She took the bottle of nard and made the most of it, right then and there (page 29).

Mary didn't set out to save the world. She simply did what she could, what was within her reach at that given moment. She used the nard to anoint his body *before* he died. What's the point of all this? What's the significance of She Did What She Could (SDWSC)? A relationship with Jesus results in a response. When we *get* that we are loved by him, we are changed from the inside out. The transformation *inside* of us changes how we live *outside* of us. We put feet on our faith.

Take a look at the following chart and consider the application question corresponding to each of these five words: *she, did, what, she, could.*

She	Who was Mary in God's sight?
Did	What did Mary do?
What	What did Mary give?
She	What was the significance of her gift?
Could	What other options might Mary have had?

CONTEMPLATE THIS

1. What do you think was most expensive for Mary — her perfume or the risk of giving it in a room of religious men in the day she lived?

2. What do you think changed for Mary as a result of her actions?

3. Why do you think Jesus chose a girl?

4. Explain what you think "A relationship with Jesus results in a response" means.

5. Why didn't one of the disciples do what Mary did?

6. Why do you think Jesus paired Mary's action with the telling of the gospel message?

7. What's the most interesting new idea for you from this lesson?

INVESTIGATE THIS

Take a look at some other examples of biblical people who did what they could.

Scripture	Who did what they could?	What did they do?	What was the result of their action?
John 6:1-13			
Luke 21:1-4			
1 Samuel 17:32-50			
Esther 4:6-17; 8:1-8			

8. How are each of these accounts alike?

9. What lessons can be learned by comparing these accounts to the account in Mark 14:3-9?

10. What biblical accounts show people doing what they could in small ways? In big ways?

11. How were these responses an outgrowth of each person's relationship with God?

RESPOND TO THIS

Visit the SDWSC website (www.sdwsc.com) to read Chrissy's story.

12. What is a recent SDWSC example you've experienced?

13. What attitude comes with SDWSC thinking?

14. Where does your relationship with Jesus fit into the SDWSC equation?

15. How do your actions demonstrate your relationship with Jesus?

16. Does SDWSC thinking need to include doing both big and small, covert and overt?

End your time by praying for opportunities in the coming week to seize SDWSC moments.

APPLY THIS

Using an index card, create a reminder for this week to put on a desktop, dashboard, fridge, etc. On one side write the letters "SDWSC." The other side should say, "A relationship with Jesus results in a response."

Commit to keeping the card in sight all week and bringing a story, written on an index card, to the next session.

Consider also posting your story on the SDWSC website (www.sdwsc.com).

Name

Date

My SDWSC Story

Who Did What She Could and Why?

Live loved.

"Knowing that Jesus receives what I do for him, in response to his love for me, as 'a beautiful thing' is helping me keep doing what I could. And in doing so, I am finding out more and more what it means to live loved." —CANDIE

B egin your time with a video clip. Visit the SDWSC website (www.sdwsc.com) and click on "Order the Book." Then click on the "This inspiring book . . ." video clip. If meeting with others, share the story you wrote this past week. Explain why that story was meaningful for you. Post your story on the storyboard.

> A storyboard is a simple way to share your stories each week if you're doing the study in a group. It can be as simple as a cardboard "display board," a bulletin board in a hallway, or even a virtual storyboard on the church website for women to add their stories each week.

CONSIDER THIS

There's more than one way to see what Mary did. Both Matthew 26:6-13 and John 12:1-8 record the same event:

> Jesus was in Bethany at the home of Simon, a man who had previously had leprosy. While he was eating, a woman came in with a beautiful alabaster jar of expensive perfume and poured it over his head.
>
> The disciples were indignant when they saw this. "What a waste!" they said. "It could have been sold for a high price and the money given to the poor."
>
> But Jesus, aware of this, replied, "Why criticize this woman for doing such a good thing to me? You will always

have the poor among you, but you will not always have me. She has poured this perfume on me to prepare my body for burial. I tell you the truth, wherever the Good News is preached throughout the world, this woman's deed will be remembered and discussed." (Matthew 26:6-13)

Six days before the Passover celebration began, Jesus arrived in Bethany, the home of Lazarus — the man he had raised from the dead. A dinner was prepared in Jesus' honor. Martha served, and Lazarus was among those who ate with him. Then Mary took a twelve-ounce jar of expensive perfume made from essence of nard, and she anointed Jesus' feet with it, wiping his feet with her hair. The house was filled with the fragrance.

But Judas Iscariot, the disciple who would soon betray him, said, "That perfume was worth a year's wages. It should have been sold and the money given to the poor." Not that he cared for the poor — he was a thief, and since he was in charge of the disciples' money, he often stole some for himself.

Jesus replied, "Leave her alone. She did this in preparation for my burial. You will always have the poor among you, but you will not always have me." (John 12:1-8)

What can we learn about this event from these two accounts?

Where was this gathering?	
Who was there?	
When did this happen?	
What were they doing?	
What's interesting about the anointing oil?	

Do we stop here, though, with just a list of the details? Let's think about what these pieces can contribute to our deeper understanding of what happened.

Mary did what she could—a daring act in front of friends and family. When you live loved, your "what" matters. Though Simon could have been just another follower of Jesus, he is more likely the elderly—and healed—father of Mary, Martha, and Lazarus. According to John 12, the criticizing voice comes from Judas Iscariot, who, known to have been greedy and a thief, helped himself to what was in the disciples' money bag. Other references indicate that some of the disciples were critical of the extravagance of Mary's act (page 4).

Where is it safer to make a risky move — in front of friends or strangers? Strangers don't know or care whether you make a fool of yourself. Family does. You'll most likely never see strangers again, but you'll likely see family often. On the other hand, acting in front of strangers can be risky as well. Will a gesture be understood or not? We don't know if Mary discussed her actions with her family ahead of time or not. Either way, she must have anticipated some of the reaction. Mary was very comfortable being with Jesus. Even when there was work to be done to help her sister, Martha, Mary chose to sit and listen to Jesus. Mary was no stranger to criticism from her sister. Martha had complained to Jesus before. In the John passage, we again see that Martha was using her serving gifts while Mary chose to use her gift of giving.

We don't know how much time Mary and the disciples had spent together. The disciples had accompanied Jesus when he raised Lazarus from the dead. Mary as well as the disciples had most likely been present when Jesus had healed Simon's leprosy. How many other times might Simon have hosted Jesus and his disciples? Did she anticipate the critical nature of Judas and the others? Had she thought through the ramifications of her extravagance?

This event took place just before Jesus' crucifixion. Mary approached Jesus with her gift of perfume and poured it out with confidence, her gesture expressing her love for him and preparing his body for burial before his death, the broken flask foreshadowing the shards customarily left in the tomb after the body's anointing for burial.[1]

While Mary couldn't know specifically that in just a few days, Jesus would be crucified, she somehow understood better than others that death was in his future. The disciples sure didn't seem to follow the unfolding reality of what lay before Jesus, but Mary innately did. And Jesus underlined her insight with his response, "She did it to prepare me for burial." The fragrance of her oil would still be discernable during Jesus' final days. Her timing, though most likely unplanned, was appropriate. What was it that Mary sensed or knew that prompted her to act so boldly at a time when she knew she would be criticized?

Mary gave with compassion and understanding. She gave from the context of who God had made her to be—and from what her relationship with him was making her. She sat at Jesus' feet, opening her soul to his teaching, his wisdom, and his love. Because she took the time to take him in, she "got" him. Over the days and months and, perhaps, years of their relationship, his investment combined with the core of her being to yield a rich essence of character, from which she later anointed him in a moment of his own great need. Spiritual intimacy had been formed, and in return, it formed her (page 23).

Mary had spent time at Jesus' feet. She'd spent enough to irritate her sister. She'd spent enough to have a heart connection

---

[1] William Barclay, *The Gospel of Mark* (Philadelphia: Wesminster, 1975), 326.

with Jesus. She may not have been able to predict exactly what was coming, but she knew there was something afoot. Mary knew enough to know his anointing was needed. She also knew enough about Jesus to know what would be meaningful. She knew he needed more than a prayer or a hug or a warm glance of encouragement. Mary also knew Jesus well enough to understand that her gift would be received and accepted by him. She may or may not have known what the reaction would be of the others in the room. But, because she was in relationship with Jesus, she knew that Jesus would receive her action as a gesture from her heart. That was enough to give her the courage to step forward and present her gift.

Mary was living loved. Because she had received love, she gave it. She understood what, so far, the disciples had missed. In this act of worship, she *lived* loved (page 23).

Mary had received Jesus' love. She knew she had to give back. She wanted to give something that was meaningful and appropriate. Mary probably had other choices: something for Jesus' continued trip to Jerusalem, making sure the chores were done before he got there, a note about her gratitude, something she'd made. Mary chose first to accept the love of Jesus. That's the main way we return God's love. There's really no greater way to love God back for his gift of Jesus. When we accept Jesus' love, it changes us and then we live differently. Mary exemplifies this. She accepted Jesus' love, and it changed her. She took time to sit at his feet and listen. She had listened enough to know what was ahead for Jesus and what would encourage him as he prepared.

When you're loved, it's easy to come up with a list of things you want to do for those who love you. Those who are loved are able to return love in meaningful ways. Mary's gift was a testament to the love she'd received. It rose up out of the context of her relationship with Jesus. After all, a relationship with Jesus results in a response. Mary did *what* she could. And when you live loved, your "what" matters.

CONTEMPLATE THIS

1. What do you think Mary was thinking and feeling as she walked into the room with her nard?

2. What do you think Mary was feeling as she poured her oil on Jesus?

3. Do you think Mary noticed what anyone else was doing while she made her offering?

4. What do you think mattered most to Mary as she offered her gift of nard?

5. How much of the significance of her actions do you think Mary was aware of?

6. What might it have been like to know Jesus as Mary did?

7. What do you think Martha's reaction might have been to this event?

INVESTIGATE THIS

There is another similar account in Luke 7:36-50, but this story is not about Mary of Bethany at all. This took place at another time and place—and with different characters—but is often confused as the same account. Take a look at this account to see what is similar and different, and note the Scripture references.

What are the differences between the two hosts?	
What are the differences between Mary and the woman in this account?	
What are the differences between the motives of the two women?	

What are the differences between Jesus' responses?	
What are the similarities between the two hosts?	
What are the similarities between Mary and the woman in this account?	
What are the similarities between the motives of the two women?	
What are the similarities between Jesus' responses?	

8. How did each woman live out of the context of her relationship with Jesus?

9. How did each woman live loved?

RESPOND TO THIS

Visit the SDWSC website (www.sdwsc.com) to read Ann's story.

10. What would be a comparable gathering in today's world?

11. What would it be like to be a guest at such a gathering if Jesus were there?

12. Would you risk giving Jesus a gift (large or small) at such a gathering?

13. Might God be inviting you to take a risk as an offering to him? How?

14. How are you like or unlike Mary?

15. What would it look like for you to give out of the context of your relationship with Jesus?

16. How might you love Jesus *back* by doing what you could?

17. How can you grow this week in your SDWSC abilities?

18. How can being a SDWSC person help you grow in your relationship with Jesus?

End your time by praying for opportunities in the coming week to seize SDWSC moments.

APPLY THIS

Using an index card, create a reminder for this week to put on a desktop, dashboard, fridge, etc. On one side write the letters "SDWSC." The other side should say, "Live loved!"

Commit to keeping the card in sight all week and bringing a story, written on an index card, to the next session.

Consider also posting your story on the SDWSC website (www.sdwsc.com).

Name

Date

My SDWSC Story

What If I Did What I Could?

How to live loved.

"I don't have to start anything big, but [just] love others one little step at a time." —ANN

Begin your time with the "Steve's Story" video clip from the SDWSC website (www.sdwsc.com). Share the story you wrote this past week. Explain why that story was meaningful for you. Post your story on the storyboard.

CONSIDER THIS

In life we live out what we believe in our hearts. God loves you. The Bible tells you so. Do you believe it? Do you live as though you believe it?

Most of us don't. We've heard God's love for us preached to us from the pulpit and piped into our iPods. We've read God's love for us in greeting cards and in Scripture verses. We've prayed God's love for us over ourselves and over those we care about. But do we really believe that God loves us to the point that we live loved?

How much does God love me? I mean really and truly. What do I really believe about the depth of God's love for me? Is what I say different from what I feel in my heart?

I'm a woman whom God loves. What if I just start there: I am loved.

I used to think such a thing was silly, immature, unnecessary. Unworthy me? Loved by God? Humph! Shame would gurgle up in my soul against such a thought. In seconds, a "shame fest" would overtake me, quietly and in secret, and I felt like a child caught in a naughty act (page 41).

What does it mean for us to take those words, "I love you," from Jesus and swallow them, digest them, and allow them to become a part of who we are? That's the beauty of Mary and what she did. She understood the depth of Jesus' love. She knew it enough to trust Jesus as she took a risk. She knew it enough to want to give back.

Consider 1 John 4:7-12 and what it says about God's love for us:

Dear friends, let us continue to love one another, for love comes from God. Anyone who loves is a child of God and knows God. But anyone who does not love does not know God, for God is love.

God showed how much he loved us by sending his one and only Son into the world so that we might have eternal life through him. This is real love—not that we loved God, but that he loved us and sent his Son as a sacrifice to take away our sins.

Dear friends, since God loved us that much, we surely ought to love each other. No one has ever seen God. But if we love each other, God lives in us, and his love is brought to full expression in us.

Use this chart to help think through what this verse is saying. Note the answers with the Scripture references.

Where does love come from?	
How do we know that God loves us?	
What do we do to receive God's love?	
How does God show his love for us in the world?	
What are we supposed to do with God's love?	

Now read verse 19: "We love each other because he loved us first." God loved us first! Before we were born, before we messed up, before we knew we needed his love, God sent Jesus to show us how much he loves us. No matter what, God loves you. Chewing on that, swallowing it, digesting it, making it fully part of your being takes a lifetime. We can all begin each day taking a new taste of God's love. Savoring this love is living loved. That's what Mary did. You and I can do it too.

Mary's action shifts me away from my shame. It's not that I deserve to be loved. I don't. She didn't. No one really does. It's just that Jesus loves me. It's a fact. When I realize that I'm not so darling in and of myself and that I don't have to be—but that I am still irrevocably loved and valued and created for good—in such moments his love becomes all the more stunning to me (page 41).

Can you accept God's love for you? I once received a challenge: spend ten minutes every day focusing on God's love for you. Really? At first the challenge rang hollow, but I decided to give it a try. For the first few days, I almost forgot. You know, I zipped through my days and suddenly remembered the challenge mid-task. So I'd stop and think about God's love, and after about thirty seconds, I lost concentration and was making a grocery list again. On about the fourth day though, just when I stopped to consider the thought that God loved me, something happened. Honest. It's as if I'd just felt God saying to me, "I love you," and then he said my name. It stunned me. I'd never heard that before: "I love you, _____."

Try it. Try ten minutes a day, focusing on this sentence: "I love you, _____," and fill in your name. You don't have to fully understand it; just take a step. Look at yourself in the mirror. That person you see is the one God sent Jesus to earth for. That person you see is the same one Jesus died for. Stunning! Try believing this thought. And then try living as though you believe this thought. That's living loved.

What might living loved look like? Mary was a pretty good example. She sat at Jesus' feet and enjoyed his presence. She didn't let the pressures of life deter her from spending time with Jesus (at least not all of the time). She trusted him enough to take risks. She knew Jesus well enough to understand what he needed.

There are some things she didn't do too. She didn't start twelve (or even one) Bible studies that we know of. She didn't sell her home and belongings to attend every appearance Jesus made. She didn't plant churches or make guest appearances at the Sanhedrin. She didn't become a nun or a martyr. Mary was Mary. She basked in Jesus' love and did what she could. That's living loved.

Living loved means that I "get" that God loves *me* and you "get" that God loves *you* and then we live out this belief in how we live by just doing what we can. It might mean sharing half my peanut butter sandwich or half my bonus. It doesn't matter. In God's eyes, the giving is the same. The half sandwich can be used to make the same eternal impact as the half bonus.

How do we know what our "what" is? How do we know the difference between one more good thing we should do and the one thing we could do that would truly make a difference? Take a look at our biblical examples. We can start small. The biblical superstars did. David was a shepherd, and so was Moses. Don't fret—you don't have to do it all perfectly. These two guys made big mistakes, and God still loved them and used them mightily as they did what they could.

Lastly, living loved means living freely and resisting our eternal self-editing that tells us that we aren't loved and can't make a difference. We can be our own worst enemy.

"Leave her alone." That's what Jesus said to the room filled with criticism. In other words, "Quit bothering her." I turn the eyes of my imagination away from Jesus and look back at Mary, seeing her the way he sees her: earnest and pure; her action in the moment, beautiful.

I am struck by his command: "Leave her alone."

Her who?

Well, Mary, of course, but also *you*.

Dear one, leave *you* alone. Leave yourself alone. Quit bothering the *her* that is *you*. Stop needling her, judging her, messing with her, being embarrassed by her. Don't tie her up in knots and make her all anxious and sweaty. Silence the stream of self-editing that tells her that she's not enough, that she's silly or worthless, that she has really bad ideas and is way out of line. Take your hands off her! Let her be (page 73–74)!

CONTEMPLATE THIS

1. What are two concrete examples of ways that God has demonstrated his love for you? Where were you? What were you doing? How did you experience God's love?

2. How would you define living loved to a twelve-year-old?

3. Let's say you and Mary were having lunch. What two questions would you ask her?

4. What are your biggest obstacles to living loved? How do you self-edit, judge, or focus on your past mistakes and then don't live loved?

5. What gifts are easiest for you to give?

6. What do you need to stop doing?

INVESTIGATE THIS

What does God's love for us look like? Let's look at a familiar Scripture passage, 1 Corinthians 13:4-8.

> Love is patient and kind. Love is not jealous or boastful or proud or rude. It does not demand its own way. It is

not irritable, and it keeps no record of being wronged. It does not rejoice about injustice but rejoices whenever the truth wins out. Love never gives up, never loses faith, is always hopeful, and endures through every circumstance.

Prophecy and speaking in unknown languages and special knowledge will become useless. But love will last forever!

This description is as much about how God loves us as it is about how we can love others.

Use this passage to answer the following questions about what is and isn't love.

What is love?	What isn't love?

7. What does this say about how God loves you?

8. What are some things God doesn't do because of his love for you?

9. What difference does God's love make?

RESPOND TO THIS

Visit the SDWSC website (www.sdwsc.com) to read Linda's story.

10. How do you receive God's love?

11. How can you be more open to God's love?

12. How does living loved help us with SDWSC living?

13. Where does SDWSC living originate?

14. Who is someone you know who lives loved well?

15. What defines a person who lives loved?

16. How will you know when you're living loved?

End your time by praying for opportunities in the coming week to seize SDWSC moments.

APPLY THIS

Using an index card, create a reminder for this week to put on a desktop, dashboard, fridge, etc. On one side write the letters "SDWSC." The other side should say, "I love you, _____ . Signed, God."

Commit to keeping the card in sight all week and bringing a story, written on an index card, to the next session.

Consider also posting your story on the SDWSC website (www.sdwsc.com).

Name

Date

My SDWSC Story

What If I Didn't Do What I Could?

Live with no regrets.

*"The phrase 'She did what she could' is set
in my mind and in my heart . . .
it has freed me in so many ways . . . to do things
I've never done and to not do things
without feeling guilty."* —NICOLE

Begin your time with "Heather's Story Part 2" from the SDWSC website (www.sdwsc.com). Share the story you wrote this past week. Explain why that story was meaningful for you. Post your story on the storyboard.

CONSIDER THIS

Peter, the "rock" on which Jesus declared he would build his church (see Matthew 16:18), and the only one brave enough to get out of the boat to walk to Jesus on the water, was undoubtedly a disciple who loved and trusted Jesus. But did he live without regrets? Take a look at what Matthew 26:37-46 says:

> He took Peter and Zebedee's two sons, James and John, and he became anguished and distressed. He told them, "My soul is crushed with grief to the point of death. Stay here and keep watch with me."
>
> He went on a little farther and bowed with his face to the ground, praying, "My Father! If it is possible, let this cup of suffering be taken away from me. Yet I want your will to be done, not mine."
>
> Then he returned to the disciples and found them asleep. He said to Peter, "Couldn't you watch with me even one hour? Keep watch and pray, so that you will not give in to temptation. For the spirit is willing, but the body is weak!"

Then Jesus left them a second time and prayed, "My Father! If this cup cannot be taken away unless I drink it, your will be done." When he returned to them again, he found them sleeping, for they couldn't keep their eyes open.

So he went to pray a third time, saying the same things again. Then he came to the disciples and said, "Go ahead and sleep. Have your rest. But look — the time has come. The Son of Man is betrayed into the hands of sinners. Up, let's be going. Look, my betrayer is here!"

Jesus had one request of his closest followers: please pray for me. And what did Peter, James, and John do? They took naps. Not once, but three times in a row. Notice that Jesus addressed Peter specifically. Pray, please. Peter didn't. He rested instead. What difference might prayer have made? Would Peter still have lopped off the guard's ear? Would he still have denied his relationship with Jesus three times? There's no way to know.

What if you *didn't* do what you could? *Ugh.* Here comes the guilt. There are so very many "she *didn't* do what she could" stories, in my life—and in yours. They point the finger of accusation at us, and we squirm in discomfort (page 51). There is one comforting reality though: I'm in good company. I have a long "didn't do" list. I didn't pray either — for my friend, my daughter, my husband, my mother. They all asked or I volunteered. But then I forgot or got busy or tired. I can think of plenty of other "didn't dos," too. Most were little things; a few were big.

When my kids were young, we visited a grandma who couldn't get out much and spent much of her time alone. We started well and then got busy and let more time pass between visits. One week my daughter repeatedly asked to visit our friend. I was too busy doing other good things. At week's end, we received word that our friend had passed away. More than twenty years later, I still regret missing our visit. I wish life had a rewind button.

What if Mary "didn't"? What if she hadn't opened her jar of nard? What if, to avoid an awkward situation, she chose to anoint Jesus later—in private—when the disciples were off doing something else? What if she decided to wait until Jesus came back after the Passover?

Jesus would still have done what he came to do. But would he have been affirmed and encouraged uniquely by Mary living loved before him, first receiving and then returning his love? If Mary had anointed him when only a few others were present, would it have been recorded? Would it have meant as much to Jesus? Would he have pronounced her action "a beautiful thing"? Would it have been an example of anything to us? Waiting a week would mean that the opportunity was lost. Fortunately, Mary did what she could when it was needed.

Does Jesus really need you and me? Will he send someone else if we "don't"? When the priest and the Levite didn't, there was the Good Samaritan. When everyone else chose otherwise, Noah chose to listen and obey. When the other sisters went home, Ruth stuck with Naomi. If Mary hadn't, would someone else have stepped in?

These questions will be answered over a cup of tea (or something better) in eternity. For now, what do I do? What if I didn't take the easy road of allowing everyone else around me to invest? What if I didn't excuse my own lack of action with the rationalization that what I could have done and didn't was really unnecessary, repetitive, or unvalued anyway? *They have enough canned food. Nobody will notice if I don't volunteer in my child's class this year. My twenty-five dollars won't make a dent.* What if instead of waiting to be invited, I jumped in, took the initiative, volunteered, offered my two widow's mites (page 49)?

If I *did* what I could, I would be acting out of God's love for me in a given moment when he has more for me to experience. More, because I move beyond considering to engaging. More, because I invest out of an attitude of caring rather than out of a sense of obligation. More, because I act instead of letting someone else act. More, because I initiate, knowing that because I *am*, I can *do*.

More, because I do instead of don't (page 53).

I'm not going to get it right all of the time. Neither are you. We're not called to live a life of guilt; we're called to live loved. When I live loved, I soak in all that God has for me as often as I can.

Welcome to the club. We all blow it. SDWSC is not about guilt avoidance. It's not about paying it forward or doing random acts of kindness or living a better life. It's not about obedience just for the sake of obedience. When I'm filled, I want to give others what I have. When I miss an opportunity, I return to God and receive his grace and mercy. I choose to spend less time on remorse, which gives me more time for giving. This is living a life with no regrets. It sounds simple, but it's not. We know better. But we can keep trying.

CONTEMPLATE THIS

1. What are some times when you wished someone would have done something (anything) and then didn't?

2. Would it have mattered to you if someone had done something for you that wasn't perfect rather than done nothing?

3. Think of a time when you didn't do something. How do you feel about it?

4. What are the consequences when we don't do what we could?

5. What difference does it really make whether we do something or not?

6. Do you think God will always find someone else to do what we didn't? Why or why not?

7. What are some other biblical examples of those who didn't do what they could?

8. What was the consequence of their inaction?

9. What should be our reason for doing something for someone else?

INVESTIGATE THIS

Read 1 John 4:17-21.

As we live in God, our love grows more perfect. So we will not be afraid on the day of judgment, but we can face him with confidence because we live like Jesus here in this world.

Such love has no fear, because perfect love expels all fear. If we are afraid, it is for fear of punishment, and this shows that we have not fully experienced his perfect love. We love each other because he loved us first.

If someone says, "I love God," but hates a Christian brother or sister, that person is a liar; for if we don't love people we can see, how can we love God, whom we cannot see? And he has given us this command: Those who love God must also love their Christian brothers and sisters.

Answer the following questions, noting the Scripture references.

What contributes to SDWSC living?	What detracts from SDWSC living?

10. What fears get in our way of doing what we can?

11. How can we find more of God's love?

12. What obstacles, fears, and inadequacies contribute to your "didn't do" list?

13. What is one fear you can confess and ask for God's help in overcoming through his love?

14. What can you do that no one has ever invited you to do?

RESPOND TO THIS

Read "Nickie's Story" from the SDWSC website (www.sdwsc.com).

15. How does Nickie's story help us see what we don't need
    to do?

16. What are some things you can do to help yourself avoid
    "didn't do" situations?

17. What can we do when we commit a "didn't do"?

18. How can we work toward a life of no regrets?

End your time by praying for opportunities in the coming week to seize SDWSC moments.

APPLY THIS

Using an index card, create a reminder for this week to put on a desktop, dashboard, fridge, etc. On one side write the letters "SDWSC." The other side should say, "Live with no regrets."

Commit to keeping the card in sight all week and bringing a story, written on an index card, to the next session.

Consider also posting your story on the SDWSC website (www.sdwsc.com).

Name

Date

My SDWSC Story

What If We Did What We Could?

You plus me equals we.

"I called my husband on the way home and he was so accepting of the fact that I'd just given our dinner away. He returned my question by asking, 'So how can I help you?' He picked up pizza on his way home from work, and we pulled in the driveway at the same time. He was smiling because we had done what we could!" —HEATHER

Open with the "Karen's Story" video clip from the SDWSC website (www.sdwsc.com). Share the story you wrote this past week. Explain why that story was meaningful for you. Post your story on the storyboard.

CONSIDER THIS

You plus me equals we. There's power in numbers. Yet often the "we" doesn't happen because someone is dis-included. Let's return to Mark 14:3-9 and see what almost happened to Mary:

> While he was in Bethany, reclining at the table in the home of Simon the Leper, a woman came with an alabaster jar of very expensive perfume, made of pure nard. She broke the jar and poured the perfume on his head.
>
> Some of those present were saying indignantly to one another, "Why this waste of perfume? It could have been sold for more than a year's wages and the money given to the poor." And they rebuked her harshly.
>
> "Leave her alone," said Jesus. "Why are you bothering her? She has done a beautiful thing to me. The poor you will always have with you, and you can help them any time you want. But you will not always have me. She did what she could. She poured perfume on my body beforehand to prepare for my burial. Truly I tell you, wherever the gospel is preached throughout the

world, what she has done will also be told, in memory of her." (NIV)

Have you ever run into people who demand that you believe everything the way they believe it or you can't be part of their "we"? Have you ever experienced what it feels like to be excluded from the great Christian "we"?

Mary nearly was. A roomful of followers collectively gasped at her action and then troubled her to the point of rejection. If the folks at that dinner party had had their way, Mary would never have acted at all, her gift of anointing Jesus' body before his death scuttled before it could even get away from the dock. But Jesus interceded. He pronounced her action beautiful and paired it with the preaching of the Good News for all time (pages 91–92).

Mary was almost dis-included. It happens. We get started on our SDWSC journey and are blindsided by naysayers: "There are starving people in Africa who need things—and deserve them—way more." "How can you rationalize spending so much time with her?" "Why are you praying instead of doing?" (Or *doing* instead of *praying*?)

If it's not the naysayers; it's those with opposing points of view. If you're focusing on marriages, you'll be criticized for not helping single parents. If you're focusing on kids, you'll be criticized for not challenging the root of the problem. If you're focusing on the political system, you'll be criticized for socializing with the wrong folks. If you're collecting for the latest natural disaster, you'll be criticized for not caring for the poor up the street.

You can probably add several more jabs—or downright opposition—just in the time since you began working your way through this study. It's easy to start thinking we're working alone. We can feel we're dragging others up our hill—on our own, in our own strength. Weariness sets in quickly.

What might happen if we turned and looked over our shoulders? How many people have our backs? Our hearts? Our spouses or our coworkers may not *always* agree with our SDWSC choices, but most of the time they're filling in for us somewhere, somehow. Our kids are learning from our example and most likely helping us. Our parents often provide childcare and a listening ear. Our friends encourage, help bring food, or take our kids. Our Bible study group prays. Or maybe you're one of the people who has someone else's back, helping them with childcare, errands, or housecleaning while they help someone else.

What might happen if we look beyond what we're doing? What if we listen to the success stories of those around us? When we listen to others who are making a difference, we're energized. We cry, we smile, we understand the victory, we rejoice. We see the bigger picture.

What if we did what we could?

We can look at the mountain ahead and become overwhelmed. Or we can look over our shoulders and see all those who are helping us, working alongside us, making positive changes in all kinds of places. You plus me equals we. There is strength in numbers. Stop, look, and rejoice in those who have joined you. Stop, look, and rejoice in those who haven't joined *you* but have joined God in another effort that matters just as much as the one you've selected.

It's vital that each one of us do what we individually could. It is also vital that we do what we could together and that we respect how others do what they could so that we are all doing what we could. We don't have to be the same to be we. We don't have to agree with each other's finer points of theology to serve a meal to the hungry. In fact, in many cases we will have less impact if we all do the same thing than we would if we each did what we could alone and then all our efforts were added to a communal *we* (page 96).

We can vote someone off the island or we can encourage each other the way we need encouragement. We can be a strong we. We can make a difference in a million different ways if we respect and encourage each other's efforts. There is so much to do. Our individual budgets are limited. We all have only twenty-four hours in a day. But together we have so much.

What could we *all* accomplish if each one of us did what she could and then *we* added all these efforts together? This is the body of Christ in action—uniquely called to both an individual and a corporate investment of who *we* are (page 90).

CONTEMPLATE THIS

1. Have you ever been dis-included?

2. Have you ever dis-included someone else?

3. Who has your back?

4. Whose back do you have?

5. Who needs you to have her back but you are resisting?

6. What effect does dis-including someone from her calling have on the bigger picture of the world's needs?

7. How could "We did what we could" thinking help accomplish more than just "I did what I could" thinking?

8. How are you involved in "We did what we could" thinking?

INVESTIGATE THIS

Read 1 Corinthians 12:12-27.

The human body has many parts, but the many parts make up one whole body. So it is with the body of Christ. Some of us are Jews, some are Gentiles, some are slaves, and some are free. But we have all been baptized into one body by one Spirit, and we all share the same Spirit.

Yes, the body has many different parts, not just one part. If the foot says, "I am not a part of the body because I am not a hand," that does not make it any less a part of the body. And if the ear says, "I am not part of the body because I am not an eye," would that make it any less a part of the body? If the whole body were an eye, how would you hear? Or if your whole body were an ear, how would you smell anything?

But our bodies have many parts, and God has put each part just where he wants it. How strange a body would be if it had only one part! Yes, there are many parts, but only one body. The eye can never say to the hand, "I don't need you." The head can't say to the feet, "I don't need you."

In fact, some parts of the body that seem weakest and least important are actually the most necessary. And the parts we regard as less honorable are those we clothe with the greatest care. So we carefully protect those parts that should not be seen, while the more honorable parts do not require this special care. So God has put the body together such that extra honor and care are given to those parts that have less dignity. This makes for harmony among the members, so that all the members care for each other. If one part suffers, all the parts suffer with it, and if one part is honored, all the parts are glad.

All of you together are Christ's body, and each of you is a part of it.

Answer the following questions with biblical references.

How are we to be like a body?	
Why aren't we all the same body part?	
How should we treat the other body parts?	

What happens to our part of the body if another part is not functioning well?	
How does Christ view the different parts of the body?	
Whose choice is it to be a particular body part?	

9. How does God desire to include all in his body?

10. Who shares your part of Christ's body?

11. How should we treat a body part that we don't agree with?

12. How do we work toward body health?

13. How does "We did what we could" thinking help foster body health?

RESPOND TO THIS

Read "Heather's Story Part 1" from the SDWSC website (www .sdwsc.com).

14. How can your family participate in SDWSC living?

15. How do you include and recognize others who are covering your back?

16. How have the times when you were dis-included shaped you?

17. How can we help each other overcome the tendency to judge others' intentions and projects?

End your time by praying for opportunities in the coming week to seize SDWSC moments.

APPLY THIS

Using an index card, create a reminder for this week to put on a desktop, dashboard, fridge, etc. On one side write the letters "SDWSC." The other side should say, "You plus me equals we."

Commit to keeping the card in sight all week and bringing a story, written on an index card, to the next session.

Consider also posting your story on the SDWSC website (www.sdwsc.com).

Name

Date

My SDWSC Story

What If We All Did What We Could?

The power of "we."

"My MOPS group knew they couldn't take away my pain from losing [my son] Ethan, but they 'did what they could' by bringing us meals, praying for us, collecting baby clothes for Grant, mowing our lawn, and so on. The group is truly a gift from God." —REBECCA

Begin with the opening video from the "Your SDWSC Stories" clip on the SDWSC website (www.sdwsc.com). Share the story you wrote this past week. Explain why that story was meaningful for you. Post your story on the storyboard.

CONSIDER THIS

Our final words to someone are often the ones we feel are most important. If you've ever sat at the bedside of someone who is dying, you know the urgency of their words. Jesus asked his disciples to meet him just before ascending to heaven, and this is what he told them:

> I have been given all authority in heaven and on earth. Therefore, go and make disciples of all the nations, baptizing them in the name of the Father and the Son and the Holy Spirit. Teaching these new disciples to obey all the commands I have given you. And be sure of this: I am with you always, even to the end of the age. (Matthew 28:18-20)

How do we go into all the nations, make disciples, and teach them how to obey what Jesus commanded? One SDWSC choice at a time. It could be with a purchased pizza, an adoption, a donation of used clothes, an encouraging word, or helping someone find the life-giving love of Jesus. It could be with hundreds of hours at a local charity, teaching a weekly Bible study, becoming a missionary, or the founding of a nonprofit. All get equal kudos from God. All are equally needed.

Individually, each action is a small drop in the bucket of worldwide needs, but collectively they fill the bucket. The power of "we" is amazing. I can't cure depression or world hunger, but I can call a friend who is feeling down and send five dollars to a relief organization. If I were the only one who did this, my two mites would still matter, but they would matter more if they were multiplied by the mites of others. When others in my small group also make a phone call and send five dollars, the effect grows. Think of the others in your community who do the same. Multiply that by the number of communities in your state, in this country. Expand your thinking to those around the world who give. It's mind boggling. It's something only God can see or orchestrate.

When we see that we're just one person among millions, when we see that we're just one part of something too big for us to comprehend—that's freeing. While my "what" matters, I don't have to do it all. I just need to do my part. I'm a part of a huge, powerful "we." I'm needed to do my part. I'm loved in spite of what I do or don't do. And so is everyone else. God chose me to do my important part. God chose you to do your important part.

You plus me equals "we," and there's great power in "we"! Can we embrace the power? We don't have to hold the same exact view of parenting to reach out and offer to unstick the plumbing in a single mom's home. We can build a well in Africa alongside those who believe that Communion should be served only by a priest. And by the way, those who receive will be blessed and want to know more. They will want to discover the source of the love we share. Those who are enlisted to help will see the love of Christ demonstrated in words and deeds. All of them could become part of the "we."

What could we all accomplish if each one of us did what we could? I might minister to moms. You might stand against abuse. He feeds the hungry. She works for justice. They advocate for the homeless. Together, we might change the world. Many acts. One we (page 96).

Some kneel in the end zone with a prayer of gratitude. Some gather their troops for a prayer of thanksgiving. Some wear a cross. Some sing worship songs while they work. Some pick up runny-nosed kids and wipe their tears while explaining God's love. Some start grassroots organizations with Christian names. Some lead Bible studies in or behind bars. The one thing they all have in common is that they're serving out of the love with which they've been filled. It's our relationship with Jesus that speaks loud and clear. It flows through our actions and our words. And when our relationship intertwines with others, it becomes a message that can't be missed. It's not a resounding gong or clanging cymbal; it's a glorious melody that both inspires and leads to the love of Jesus and then to the nations of the world.

She did what she could. One girl entered a relationship with Jesus, and because a relationship with Jesus results in a response, she did what she could. She lived loved. Jesus invites us to do the same. He beckons us to a relationship with him, a relationship that results in a response, an action. Going. Doing. Giving. Loving. When we know Jesus and are known by him, we can live loved—all of us. Individually and together. You. And me. *We*.

What if . . . *we* did what *we* could (page 97)?

CONTEMPLATE THIS

1. How is God's love revealed in your SDWSC actions?

2. How could you include others in your SDWSC actions?

3. Who in your circle of influence has heard the Good News as a result of your SDWSC actions?

4. When have you seen a small piece of the power of "we" in action?

5. Who do you know who needs to hear the Good News through an SDWSC choice?

6. How does Jesus' love naturally flow through you?

7. What's the most inspiring SDWSC story you've heard? Why is it so inspiring to you?

INVESTIGATE THIS

Read 1 Peter 3:13-18 and think about the hope that is within you:

Who will want to harm you if you are eager to do good? But even if you suffer for doing what is right, God will reward you for it. So don't worry or be afraid of their threats. Instead, you must worship Christ as Lord of your life. And if someone asks about your Christian hope, always be ready to explain it. But do this in a gentle and respectful way. Keep your conscience clear. Then if people speak against you, they will be ashamed when they see what a good life you live because you belong to Christ. Remember, it is better to suffer for doing good, if that is what God wants, than to suffer for doing wrong!

Christ suffered for our sins once for all time. He never sinned, but he died for sinners to bring you safely home to God. He suffered physical death, but he was raised to life in the Spirit.

Look through the passage for the answers to each of the following questions.

What should you always be prepared for?	
What is there to fear?	
What is it best to suffer for?	
How are we to give our testimonies?	
Why should we be ready to give a testimony?	

8. What is your source of hope?

9. When others ask you about your source of hope, what do you say?

10. What do you fear when it comes to sharing your testimony?

11. How does your hope help fuel the power of "we"?

RESPOND TO THIS

Read "Rebecca's Story" from the SDWSC website (www.sdwsc .com).

12. How can you share SDWSC with someone else this week?

13. What has been the most important lesson you've learned from this SDWSC study?

14. How has SDWSC thinking helped you with your testimony?

End your time by praying for opportunities in the coming week to seize SDWSC moments.

APPLY THIS

Using an index card, create a reminder for this week to put on a desktop, dashboard, fridge, etc. On one side write the letters

"SDWSC." The other side should say, "What if we did what we could?"

Commit to keeping the card in sight all week.

Consider posting your story on the SDWSC website (www.sdwsc.com).

Name

Date

My SDWSC Story

About the Author

Elisa Morgan was named by *Christianity Today* as one of the top fifty women influencing today's church and culture, and she's a sought-after author, speaker, and leader. She has authored more than twenty-five books on mothering, spiritual formation, and evangelism, including *The Beauty of Broken*; *Hello, Beauty Full*; *She Did What She Could*; and the *Mom's Devotional Bible* (NIV).

For twenty years, Elisa served as the CEO of MOPS International (www.mops.org). Under her leadership, MOPS grew from 350 groups to more than 4,000 groups throughout the United States and in thirty other countries, influencing more than one hundred thousand moms every year. Elisa now serves as president emerita of MOPS.

Elisa received a BS from the University of Texas and an MDiv from Denver Seminary. She served as the dean of women at Western Bible College (now Colorado Christian University) and on the board of the Evangelical Council for Financial Accountability. Currently, she serves on the board of Denver Seminary.

Elisa is a cohost of the syndicated radio program *Discover the Word* (www.discovertheword.org)—a daily fifteen-minute real-time conversation around the living Word of God. She is married to Evan (the senior vice president of global ministry efforts for Our Daily Bread Ministries) and has two grown children and two grandchildren who live near her in Denver, Colorado. Wilson and Darla, her two Rottweilers, take her on walks in the open space behind her house.

Connect with Elisa at www.elisamorgan.com. You can sign up to receive updates for her blog, *Really*, at her website or by texting the word *REALLY* to 22828.

You can keep in touch with Elisa in the following ways:

Instagram: @ElisaMorganAuthor
Facebook: Elisa Morgan, Author
Twitter: @elisa_morgan

Want more of what you've read here?

---

elisamorgan.com

Sign up to receive Elisa's blog posts.

Book Elisa to speak for your event.

Listen to Elisa on discovertheword.org.

Follow Elisa
on Facebook and Instagram
@ElisaMorganAuthor
and on Twitter
@elisa_morgan.

Elisa Morgan
Really

Living really ... Really living

CP1326